The Descartes Dictionary

ALSO AVAILABLE FROM BLOOMSBURY

The Bloomsbury Philosophy Dictionaries offer clear and accessible guides to the work of some of the more challenging thinkers in the history of philosophy. A–Z entries provide clear definitions of key terminology, synopses of key works, and details of each thinker's major themes, ideas, and philosophical influences. The Dictionaries are the ideal resource for anyone reading or studying these key philosophers.

The Deleuze and Guattari Dictionary, Eugene B. Young with Gary Genosko and Janell Watson

The Derrida Dictionary, Simon Morgan Wortham

The Gadamer Dictionary, Chris Lawn and Niall Keane

The Hegel Dictionary, Glenn Alexander Magee

The Husserl Dictionary, Dermot Moran and Joseph Cohen

The Kant Dictionary, Lucas Thorpe

The Marx Dictionary, Ian Fraser and Lawrence Wilde

The Merleau-Ponty Dictionary, Donald A. Landes

The Nietzsche Dictionary, Douglas Burnham

The Sartre Dictionary, Gary Cox

BLOOMSBURY PHILOSOPHY DICTIONARIES

The Descartes Dictionary

KURT SMITH

Bloomsbury Academic
An imprint of Bloomsbury Publishing Plc

B L O O M S B U R Y
LONDON · NEW DELHI · NEW YORK · SYDNEY

Bloomsbury Academic
An imprint of Bloomsbury Publishing Plc

50 Bedford Square	Bloomsbury Publishing	1385 Broadway
London	Ireland, 29 Earlsfort	New York
WC1B 3DP	Terrace, Dublin 2, D02	NY 10018
UK	AY28, Ireland	USA

www.bloomsbury.com

Bloomsbury and the Diana logo are trademarks of Bloomsbury Publishing Plc

First published 2015

© Kurt Smith, 2015

Kurt Smith has asserted his right under the Copyright, Designs and Patents Act, 1988, to be identified as Author of this work.

All rights reserved. No part of this publication may be: i) reproduced or transmitted in any form, electronic or mechanical, including photocopying, recording or by means of any information storage or retrieval system without prior permission in writing from the publishers; or ii) used or reproduced in any way for the training, development or operation of artificial intelligence (AI) technologies, including generative AI technologies. The rights holders expressly reserve this publication from the text and data mining exception as per Article 4(3) of the Digital Single Market Directive (EU) 2019/790.

Bloomsbury Publishing Plc does not have any control over, or responsibility for, any third-party websites referred to or in this book. All internet addresses given in this book were correct at the time of going to press. The author and publisher regret any inconvenience caused if addresses have changed or sites have ceased to exist, but can accept no responsibility for any such changes.

British Library Cataloguing-in-Publication Data
A catalogue record for this book is available from the British Library.

ISBN: HB: 978-1-4725-1469-1
PB: 978-1-4725-1010-5
ePDF: 978-1-4725-1244-4
ePub: 978-1-4725-0726-6

Library of Congress Cataloging-in-Publication Data
Smith, Kurt, 1961- author.
The Descartes dictionary / Kurt Smith.
pages cm. – (Bloomsbury philosophy dictionaries)
Includes bibliographical references and index.
ISBN 978-1-4725-1469-1 (hardback) –
ISBN 978-1-4725-1010-5 (paperback) – ISBN 978-1-4725-0726-6 (epub)
1. Descartes, Ren?, 1596-1650–Dictionaries. I. Title.
B1831.S65 20159780520238145
194–dc23
2014021232

Typeset by Newgen Knowledge Works (P) Ltd., Chennai, India
Printed and bound in India

Contents

Acknowledgments vi
About this dictionary vii

Introduction 1
    A sketch of Descartes's life 1
    A sketch of Descartes's philosophical system 5
    Descartes in the classroom 24

Terms and names 29

Bibliography 123

Acknowledgments

I thank Colleen Coalter, Commissioning Editor in philosophy for Bloomsbury Publishing, who first approached me about doing this project, and who has been instrumental from beginning to end. I also thank Andrew Wardell who helped guide me through much of the pre-printing process. And, I thank my copy editor, Srikanth Srinivasan, for the careful read. Decisions on which entries to include, on which to expand, on which to contract, and so on were made with the help of anonymous readers. So, I thank them (whoever and wherever they are!). For some of the details included in the Introduction, especially in the section titled "Descartes in the Classroom," I thank Roger Ariew, Fred Beiser, John Carriero, Michael Della Rocca, Daniel Garber, Stephen Gaukroger, Nicholas Griffin, Andrew Janiak, Thomas Lennon, Terry Meyers, Ray Monk, Steven Nadler, Alan Nelson, Elizabeth Radcliffe, and Alison Simmons. They thoughtfully responded to queries about their earliest exposures to Descartes's work as students, and several were able to tell me about the use of Descartes in the classroom during the seventeenth, eighteenth, and nineteenth centuries. Lastly, I thank the artists, Eleanor Rose and Rebecca Cobb, who prepared the cover. Each dictionary in the series includes on its cover an important "object" that is usually associated with the philosopher (whose work the dictionary is about). I chose the tree, since it was an important image for Descartes. In the Preface to the *Principles* (the French version), he writes: "Thus the whole of philosophy is like a tree. The roots metaphysics, the trunk is physics, and the branches emerging from the trunk are all the other sciences, which may be reduced to three principal ones, namely medicine, mechanics, and morals" (AT IXB 14; CSM I 186).

About this dictionary

This dictionary has been geared specifically for undergraduate students. The terms and philosophical concepts included are those that have typically proven difficult for students coming to Descartes's writings for the first time.

Descartes's philosophical career spanned almost his entire adult life. He was a living, breathing human being, warts and all. We need to remind ourselves of this because human beings, real human beings, change and grow. This includes what they think about, how they think about those things, and so on. It would be unreasonable, then, when examining the entire span of Descartes's philosophical writings to expect to find a single, unified, perfectly consistent view. We must allow for the likelihood of a change in mind. It would be equally unreasonable to expect to find just one set of terms whose meanings remained the same over that same span of work. An important aim of this dictionary is to track these sorts of changes if and when they occur.

There are two principles that have guided the composition of the entries to follow. Both are important to doing the history of philosophy. The first is what we might call the *principle of fidelity*. This principle requires that we be *faithful* to the texts. The texts are what they are, and we must be mindful to present them as accurately as possible. The second principle is what we might call the *principle of charity*. This principle requires that we be *charitable* to the view under investigation. This second principle can be trickier to apply than the first. Suppose, for instance, that there are two ways of reading or interpreting a text. Clearly, the principle of fidelity requires that we be faithful to the text. But in this case, there are at least two ways of understanding the text (in other words, there is an inherent ambiguity). Which way of reading the text do we adopt? The principle of charity requires us to adopt the way that is most charitable to

Descartes. Thus, if one way of reading the text puts Descartes into conflict with other things he says, while the other way of reading the text puts him in line with those other things, the principle of charity, assuming that it is important that Descartes be consistent on the point in question, requires us to adopt the second reading, the one that puts him in line with other things he says.

When provoked by critics, Descartes (on occasion) admits that he was using certain philosophical terms differently from how they were used in the Schools. Johannes Caterus (1590–1657), for example, author of the First Set of Objections of the *Meditations*, expressed concerns over what he took to be Descartes's odd use of certain terms. He asks Descartes, for instance, to explain what he had meant by the terms "idea," "objective being," and "nothing." Later in the First Set of Objections, he expresses concern over Descartes's use of "real distinction." Caterus complains that Descartes uses these terms very differently from the way the Schools used them. Descartes's replies to such critics are not always that illuminating, for he will sometimes simply shrug off the concern, or simply admit that he is using a term differently than it had been used by others. Even so, he usually says enough in other places that allow us to figure out what he meant by the term in question. In light of this, where appropriate, the then-standard usage of a term will be noted in an entry, so as to help the reader better understand the import of Descartes's change in its usage.

Since Descartes wrote almost exclusively in Latin and in French (though he wrote some letters in Dutch), it is sometimes helpful to the English reader to see the actual words he used. To this end, when helpful, this dictionary will include the Latin and French terms that Descartes actually used. They will be provided directly following the term to be defined, and in many cases they will appear in the entry itself. Concerning "definitions," it should be noted that it is rare that a one-liner will suffice. In many cases, if not most, determining what a term means requires some discussion of other texts. Even in cases where Descartes provides an actual definition, simply repeating it will not be enough to understand the full *philosophical* import of the term defined. So, the reader should think of each entry not so much as a definition proper, but as a discussion of the term in question.

ABOUT THIS DICTIONARY

The following entries are based entirely on Descartes's writings—on the actual texts. Even so, the entries have been informed (and improved!) by looking to the secondary literature. It is worth noting that a careful study of the secondary literature reveals that there is, not surprisingly, no ultimate consensus on Descartes's views. Rather, one finds many interesting interpretations in scholarly competition with one another. With this in mind, and in trying to provide the reader with some sense of the array of interpretations available, the relevant secondary literature has been incorporated into certain entries, these influences provided at the end of each entry. But even here, these references are not definitive. They are only suggestions about where one might begin the next step in one's research.

Descartes employed a number of distinctions that together formed much of the foundation of his philosophical system. For example, he employed the distinction between *a posteriori* and *a priori*, the distinction between the *analytic* and the *synthetic* methods, the distinction between *formal reality* and *objective reality*, to name only three. To make things easier for the reader, this dictionary handles a *distinction* as a single entry. Thus, the reader will find *a posteriori* and *a priori* together as one entry, *analysis* and *synthesis* together as one entry, and so on. Descartes also couples certain concepts. When dealing with ideas, for example, Descartes couples *clarity* and *distinctness*, and *obscurity* and *confusion*. The former and latter couplings form part of an important distinction. Thus, the entire block of related concepts is handled in a single entry.

The reader will notice that some of the entries include bits and pieces from other entries. This was done so that readers would not have to bounce back and forth between related entries.

Lastly, there is a collection of Descartes's works, which includes five volumes of correspondence, that has become a central body of reference for scholars. This is the 11-volume 1897 collection put together by Charles Adam and Paul Tannery, typically referred to as the "Adam and Tannery" volumes. When citing Descartes's works, this dictionary will make reference to this collection as "AT," which will be followed by the volume and page numbers. Whenever possible, this dictionary also uses the now-famous

ABOUT THIS DICTIONARY

English translations of John Cottingham, Robert Stoothoff, and Dugald Murdoch, which is in three volumes. Relatively recently, letters translated by Anthony Kenny were included in volume three. When citing this three-volume set this dictionary will use "CSM," and for volume three, "CSMK," followed by the appropriate volume and page numbers. The AT and CSM citations will be put side by side, separated by a semicolon.

Introduction

A sketch of Descartes's life

René Descartes was born on March 31, 1596, to Joachim Descartes and Jeanne Brochard, in the small town of La Haye, France. To put this into some context consider the fact that the year Descartes was born Queen Elisabeth I of England would have been 63 years old, both Galileo and Shakespeare would have been 32, Kepler would have been 25, Hobbes would have been 8, and Pocahontas would have been 1. Descartes's father was a lawyer and magistrate, serving in the Parliament of Brittany in Rennes. His mother died the year following his birth, at which time he and his brother and sister, Pierre and Jeanne, were sent to live with their maternal grandmother. At the age of 10, in 1606, Descartes was enrolled in the Jesuit college of La Flèche. He completed his studies there in 1614, entering law school at the Université de Poitiers. In 1616, he received his Baccalaureate and License in Canon and Civil Law.

Instead of entering the practice of law, Descartes, like many young men of his day, entered military service—but he did not join the French army as one might expect, but instead joined the army of the Dutch Prince, Maurice of Nassau. He was stationed in Breda. This was in 1618. There he met Isaac Beeckman (1588–1637), a Dutch physician and teacher. They became friends and it is Beeckman who appears to have rekindled in Descartes an interest in the sciences and mathematics. As a result of their philosophical discussions, Descartes produced the *Compendium Musicae* (*Compendium on Music*). In this work, Descartes casts music (or perhaps better, music theory) in physical, and ultimately in mathematical, terms. Even so, it would not be published during his lifetime.

After leaving the army, we lose track of Descartes, though he does tell us (in the *Discourse on the Method*) that in 1619 he had attended the Coronation of Ferdinand II in Frankfurt, Germany. Some have speculated that he visited Italy during this "lost" period. We know for sure that he emerges in Paris in 1625, and is immediately at the center of the intellectual scene, where he became good friends with a priest, one Marin Mersenne (1588–1648), a member of a rather eccentric order, the Order of Minims. Descartes would come to rely heavily on Mersenne, especially during the writing and production stages of some of his major philosophical works.

Descartes leaves Paris for the Netherlands around 1628. He tells Mersenne that he is working on several things, which in the end will constitute a larger work. He tentatively titles it *The World*. In 1632 or so, it is ready for publication. But in learning of Galileo's 1633 conflict with Church authorities, Descartes pulls *The World* from the presses. It is not published during his lifetime. What he does is salvage some of the smaller treatises that made up *The World*, and begins to reconfigure them so as to avoid conflict with Church authorities. Two of the "little treatises," as he refers to them in letters, are very likely what he later titles the *Optics* and the *Meteorology*. Another possibly related treatise is the *Treatise on Man*. By around 1634 or so, Descartes says that he is putting together a short work that will depict the basics of his method.

He pitches the title of this short work in a letter to Mersenne: *The Plan of a Universal Science which is capable of raising our nature to its highest degree of perfection. In addition, the Optics, the Meteorology, and the Geometry, in which the Author, in order to give proof of his universal Science, explains the most abstruse Topics he could choose, and does so in such a way that even persons who have never studied can understand them.* Mersenne was able to talk him out of this rather long title, and got him to accept a shorter one. Today, the work is known simply as the *Discourse*, which is short for *Discourse on the Method*. The three attached essays, the *Optics*, the *Meteorology*, and the *Geometry*, are appended so as to demonstrate how the method briefly discussed in the *Discourse* was supposed to work. It was originally published anonymously in 1637.

It is not clear how the three essays demonstrate Descartes's "method." The *Geometry* looks to have been in the works since

1618, and is mentioned by Descartes in letters to Beeckman. In the *Geometry*, Descartes makes interesting and important connections between Euclidean geometry and algebra. In short, he "translates" geometry into algebra and vice versa. This allowed him to take difficult geometrical problems, to translate them into algebra, and then to solve them using algebraic rules. It was this connection that in part made possible the next step in the development of a "mathematical" physics, which emerges a generation later in Isaac Newton (1643–1727) and others. We also find the beginnings of a new conception of matter, as simply extension in length, breadth, and depth, in these essays, where physics (or natural philosophy as it was called back then) dealt with bodies understood simply as extended things, which were shaped and in motion. Descartes played a crucial part in establishing this. The *Discourse* was a smashing success.

A few years later, Descartes began to work up a "textbook" for the Schools. This turned out to be his now famous *Meditations on First Philosophy*, or what is simply referred to as the *Meditations*. It was published in 1641. Mersenne was able to interest several people in reading and offering objections to the *Meditations*. Among these were Thomas Hobbes (1588–1679), Antoine Arnauld (1612–94), Pierre Gassendi (1592–1655), and Mersenne himself. Mersenne looks to have also gathered together objections from several anonymous critics, and included those along with his own objections. Descartes was then given a chance to reply to the objections. When all was said and done, the *Meditations* was published along with the appended "Objections and Replies." There were six sets of objections and replies in the first printing, and seven in the second printing.

In the *Meditations*, Descartes introduces his epistemology and metaphysics. His epistemology, or *theory of knowledge*, was a direct challenge to skepticism, the view that knowledge is impossible. His metaphysics, or theory of what there "really" is, works to establish what is now referred to as *Cartesian dualism* (where "Cartesian" simply refers to Descartes's name—which used to be spelled *Des Cartes*. The term "dualism" is telling, since it denotes, in "dual," the number two). Descartes held that there were at bottom only two kinds of finite substances: *minds* and *bodies*. One of the hidden aims of the *Meditations*, according to what Descartes tells Mersenne in a letter, is to overthrow the then dominant versions of Aristotelian physics. The latter were grounded in the qualities hot, cold, wet, and dry. By the Third Meditation, Descartes is able to call into question our ideas of these qualities, casting them in terms of their being materially false. The only principles on which to base any physics are the ones he proposes: extended things that are shaped, sized, in motion, and so on.

The next major work was the *Principles of Philosophy*, usually referred to as the *Principles*. It is a large work, four parts with over 500 articles. It was published in 1644. In it Descartes begins with a quick run-through of his epistemology and metaphysics, which, with a few exceptions, very closely follows the program as developed in the *Meditations*. He then moves to Part II, and deals primarily with body, motion, and the laws of motion. In Parts III and IV he provides real-world application, addressing issues related to astronomy, physics, and the like. He says that he wanted to include a part on living things (biology) and another on man (very likely focused on human anatomy and physiology), but hints that he had simply run out of time. Had he completed the *Principles* to include these things, the *Principles* would have very likely looked like *The World*.

An important correspondent of Descartes's, Princess Elisabeth (of Bohemia), began to press Descartes on problems that she found lurking in his metaphysics. Elisabeth's criticism appears to assume that causal interaction required the possibility of contact. Assuming this, and that the natures of minds and bodies are as Descartes says, then no account of how minds and bodies *causally* interact will be possible. Her criticism went something like this. Clearly, all finite bodies will have shapes, which means that they will have surfaces. In fact, it is by way of their surfaces that bodies will be able to come into contact with one another. Now, it will also be true that if something has a surface (coextensive with its shape), it will be extended. But, a mind, according to Descartes, is essentially a thinking thing, and essentially *not* extended. At least this is what he had said in the Synopsis of the *Meditations* and in the Sixth Mediation. If a mind is not extended, it follows that it does not (and cannot) have a surface. But if it does not have a surface, it cannot in principle come into contact with anything (neither can anything come into contact with it). If there is no way for the body to come into contact with the mind, and there is no way for the mind to come into contact with the body, then causal interaction looks to be utterly impossible.

After thinking much about the sort of criticism that Elisabeth leveled against his view, Descartes believed that he could provide some response, and he put that in a new work, titled the *Passions of the Soul*. It was published in 1649, the year, in fact, Descartes had joined the court of Queen Christina (of Sweden). It was the last work Descartes would ever publish. For, as it would turn out, things took a bad turn for him in Sweden. He did not like his new position, which among other things required him to tutor the Queen in philosophy, from five to about ten most mornings. Another one of his responsibilities seems to have been the designing of a new school or university. Descartes says in correspondence that he did not like the cold weather, and likens the intellectual environment of the court to the frozen landscape. In late January or early February of 1650, Descartes fell ill. From some descriptions, it would appear that he had acquired a serious respiratory infection. Early in the morning of February 11, 1650, Descartes succumbed to the infection and died there in Stockholm. He was only 53 years old.

A sketch of Descartes's philosophical system

In the Preface to the French edition of the *Principles of Philosophy* (1647), Descartes says: "the whole of philosophy is like a tree. The roots are metaphysics, the trunk is physics, and the branches emerging from the trunk are all the other sciences, which may be reduced to three principal ones, namely medicine, mechanics, and morals" (AT IXB 14; CSM I 186). The tree is an analogy meant to emphasize the unity of the sciences. *Scientia*, which is the Latin word that Descartes uses, was taken by philosophers of the period to refer to a *systematic* body of knowledge. A paradigm example of such a system was Euclid's geometry. Such a system first established definitions, from which axioms were made. The latter were self-evidently true (given the definitions). From the axioms and certain postulates, all other theorems and specific geometrical propositions could be derived. Such a system formed a hierarchical, interrelated "web" of propositions, the system ultimately grounded in first principles (the axioms). Metaphysics, as Descartes tells us in the *Principles* passage just quoted, occupies an important place in the system. All sciences ultimately stem from and are nourished by it. It is no wonder that philosophers of the period, including Descartes, took the study of metaphysics to be a study of what they called "first philosophy." In fact, the full title of the *Meditations*—*Meditations on First Philosophy* (1641)—makes clear to the reader that the work is principally a study in metaphysics. Let's now look briefly at each part of Descartes's *scientia*, beginning with its "roots"—the metaphysics.

Descartes's metaphysics: The roots

One aim of the metaphysics is to establish what counts as "real"— specifically, what counts as the true entities that constitute the universe, those basic entities that underlie all other entities, which account for the very *possibility* of everything else. It is a study of what there "really," or fundamentally, is. Such a theory is called an *ontology*. The ancient Greek word "*ontos*" means *being*. So, roughly speaking, an ontology is a theory of being. Descartes took there to be two *kinds* of being, which as often as not he refers to as two kinds of "reality": *formal reality* and *objective reality*. Of the two, formal reality was more fundamental insofar as objective reality ultimately depended on it. According to Descartes, formal reality is the kind of reality a thing possesses in virtue of its being an *existent* (or *actual*) thing. So, for example, insofar as the Sun exists (i.e., is actual), it possesses formal reality. By contrast, insofar as Pegasus does not exist (i.e., is not actual), it does not possess formal reality. The Sun is a formal being and Pegasus is not. Objective reality, on the other hand, was taken to be the kind of reality a thing possesses in virtue of its being a *representation* of something. As we will see, Descartes took ideas to be the only items in his ontology that possessed this kind of reality.

There are three "levels" of (formal and objective) reality: the level of that of an *infinite substance*, the level of that of a *finite substance*, and the level of that of a *mode*. The level of formal reality of an infinite substance, for instance, is greater than that of a finite substance, and the level of formal reality of a finite substance is greater than that of a mode. Alternatively, in respect to formal reality, this can be understood in terms of ontological dependence. For example, the level of formal reality of a mode is less than that of a finite substance insofar as a mode depends for its being (its formal reality) on the being (formal reality) of a finite substance in a way that the being (formal reality) of a finite substance does not depend for its being (formal reality) on the being (formal reality) of a mode. The same holds for the relationship between a finite substance and an infinite substance. The level of formal reality of a finite substance is less than that of an infinite substance insofar as a finite substance depends for its being (its formal reality) on the being (formal reality) of an infinite substance in a way that the being (formal reality) of an infinite substance does not depend for its being (formal reality) on the being (formal reality) of a finite substance. This is the sense in which an infinite substance is said to be more real than a finite substance, and a finite substance is said to be more real than a mode.

A substance is something that can exist independently of anything else. Strictly speaking, Descartes says in the *Principles*, there is only one thing that meets this criterion, namely God. So, strictly speaking, there is only one substance. On Descartes's view, God is *the* infinite substance (so, there is no possibility of there being more than one). Finite substances, though called "substances," cannot exist independently of the infinite substance, and so strictly speaking they are not substances. Even so, there are two basic (kinds of) finite beings that can exist independently of one another, namely *mind* and *body*. So, in the sense that they can exist independently of one another, Descartes says that we can refer to them as (finite) substances, though we must always keep it in mind that they are not substances in the full-blown or strict sense.

Each of the two (kinds of) finite substances is defined by what Descartes calls its "principal attribute." The principal attribute of a thing is its essence or nature. Along the lines of ancient Greek philosophy, the essence or nature of a thing was taken to be some property or collection of properties that defined the thing as being the kind of thing it was. So, if for any object x, x is an instance of kind k whenever x possesses property p, then, if the essence or nature of *x* is *k* (i.e., what it is to be *x* is to be an instance of kind *k*), *x* possesses *p*. In other words, anything whose essence or nature is *k* possesses *p*. Take, for example, a Euclidian triangle *T*. For *T* to be this kind of thing (a Euclidean triangle), one property that *T* must have is that its interior angles equal the sum of two right angles. If *T*'s interior angles do not equal the sum of two right angles, then *T* is not (and cannot be) a Euclidean triangle. Descartes took the essence or nature of mind to be *thought* (or *thinking*) and the essence or nature of body to be *extension* (specifically in length, breadth, and depth). So, the principal attribute of mind is thought, and the principal attribute of body is extension. If something does not think, it isn't a mind; if something is not extended, it isn't a body.

Each finite substance, as defined by its principal attribute, can be modified. Such a modification is what Descartes calls a "mode." A mode is *a way of being* a finite substance. A *shape* is a mode of body. Specifically, a shape is a way of being extended. It is a way in which an instance of extension is manifested. Likewise, *doubting* is a mode of mind. Specifically, doubting is a way of being thought. It is a way in which an instance of thought (or thinking) is manifested. Notice the logical or conceptual relationship between a mode and the attribute of which it is a modification. If we think of a shaped thing, for instance, we must be thinking of an extended thing. A shaped–unextended thing is plainly and simply inconceivable (i.e., it's a contradiction). As Descartes puts it in the *Principles*, "Everything else which can be attributed to body presupposes extension, and is merely a mode of an extended thing . . . For example, shape is unintelligible except in an extended thing . . ." (AT VIIIA 25; CSM I 210). Even so, he goes on to say, we can conceive of extension without conceiving a shape. The conceptual or logical asymmetry between *shape* and *extension* suggests: *shape entails extension* (but not vice versa). The same holds between modes of mind and its principal attribute thought. If we think of a thing as something that is at the moment doubting something, we must be thinking of this thing as engaged in an act of thinking. But, we certainly can think of something that is thinking (perhaps it is affirming something) and yet not think of it as something that is at the moment doubting something. This suggests: *doubting entails thinking* (but not vice versa). Thus, *shape* is to *extension* as *doubt* is to *thought*.

Since Descartes's ontology holds that there are fundamentally only two kinds of finite substance in the universe, mind and body, his metaphysics is counted as a form of *dualism* ("dual" indicates *two*). He establishes his dualism by first showing that mind and body are really distinct. *Real distinction* is an important component of Descartes's metaphysics. We can define it thus: *A* and *B* are *really distinct* if, and only if, we can conceive of the nature of *A* completely independently of our conceiving the nature of *B*, and vice versa. Descartes argues that by showing that *A* and *B* are really distinct, we have shown that they can exist independently of one another. In this way, we might take *A* and *B* to be two distinct substances (in the qualified sense noted earlier). Consider again the relationship between shape and extension. In the previous paragraph, we noted that shape entails extension. This means that in every case in which something is shaped (or we conceived something as shaped), it is extended (or we conceived of that something as extended). The logic here is straightforward. If something was not extended, it could not be shaped. We cannot conceive shape completely independently of our conceiving extension. Since this is so, shape is not really distinct from extension. As Descartes will put it, shape is only *modally* distinct from extension. The same holds for doubt. If something is not thinking, it cannot be doubting. We cannot conceive doubt (or doubting) completely independently of our conceiving thought (or thinking). Doubt is only *modally* distinct from thought. They are not really distinct from one another. But when we consider the natures of mind and body, Descartes argues that we *can* conceive them completely independently of one another.

Thus, when we conceive of the nature of body, which is extension, we need not think of it as thinking. Consider, for example, a table, which in being a body is by its very nature extended. Insofar as it is conceived as having a shape, size, and so on, we conceive the table as extended. But we need not (and typically do not) conceive bodies such as tables as being things that think. This shows, Descartes claims, that we can conceive of a body (its nature) completely independently of conceiving a mind (its nature). Similarly, he argues, when we conceive of the nature of mind, which is thought or thinking, we need not conceive of the mind as extended. Since the natures of mind and body can be conceived completely independently of one another, mind and body are really distinct (from one another). In this sense, they can be understood as possibly existing independently of one another, and so (in the qualified sense) can be called (created or finite) *substances*.

Ideas (as a component of the metaphysics)

It was noted earlier that *ideas* are the only items in Descartes's ontology that possess objective reality. This kind of reality, recall, is the reality a thing possesses in virtue of its *representing* something. So, ideas represent things to the mind, and they do so by way of their possessing objective reality. Now, ideas, insofar as they *exist*, must also possess formal reality. Since ideas are modes of mind, they possess only the lowest "level" of formal reality (the level of that of a mode). "The nature of an idea," Descartes says, "is such that of itself it requires no formal reality except what it derives from my thought, of which it is a mode" (AT VII 41; CSM II 28). So, the formal reality of an idea has its origin in the formal reality of the mind, of which it is a mode. But what about objective reality? Descartes says: "But in order for a given idea to contain such and such objective reality, it must surely derive it from some cause which contains at least as much formal reality as there is objective reality in the idea. For if we suppose that an idea contains something which was not in its cause, it must have got this from nothing . . ." (AT VII 41; CSM II 28–9). Of course, something cannot come from nothing, so if something is contained in an idea, the idea must have got this from some cause. To be sure, Descartes admits, the objective reality of one idea may have its origin in the objective reality of another. But, he is quick to assert, "there cannot be an infinite regress here; eventually one must reach a primary idea, the cause of which will be like an archetype which contains formally <and in fact> all the reality <or perfection> which is present only objectively <or representatively> in the idea" (AT VII 42; CSM II 29). Ultimately, the objective reality of what he calls our *primary ideas* must have its origin in the formal reality of some object—which when not the mind will be an object that exists external to, or independently of, the mind.

In the Third Meditation, Descartes makes a close examination of his ideas. When considered in terms of their formal reality (or being), that is, as existent modes, they all appear to be similar and "there is no recognizable inequality among them" (AT VII 40; CSM II 27). But, when considered in terms of their objective reality (or being), that is, in terms of their representational content, "they differ widely" (AT VII 40; CSM II 28). Although there are some important dissimilarities with the following analogy, use of it can be of some help in making some of this clearer.

Consider a case of several photographs placed side by side on a table. We measure each photograph and note that each is the same size (let's say each is 5 inches by 7 inches); we weigh each photograph and note that each weighs the same; we run our fingers over the surface of each and note that each feels the same (each is smooth to the touch); and so on. As Descartes might put it: there is no recognizable difference between them. But things are different when considering them in respect to their content. For example, one photograph represents the Empire State Building, while another represents Abraham Lincoln. Here, in respect to their representational content, the photographs differ widely. Let the properties of the photograph, the ones that are attributed solely to the photograph understood as a thing *sans* any consideration of its representational content—so only consider its size, shape, weight, and so on—be analogs to the formal being of an idea. For lack of a better name, we'll call these the formal properties of the photograph. By contrast, let the properties of the photograph, the ones that we're associating with its representing something (or, perhaps better, with its representational content) *sans* any consideration of the photograph's size, shape, weight, and so on (i.e., *sans* any consideration of its formal properties), be analogous to the objective reality of our ideas. We'll call these the objective properties of the photograph. In light of the photograph analogy, Descartes's theory of ideas suggests the following. Suppose someone points at one of the photographs and asks, "How tall is this?" Suppose that the photograph in question is the photograph of the Empire State Building. There are two possible answers to the question. If we take our inquirer to be referring to a formal property of the photograph, then the right answer looks to be: "It is seven inches tall." But, if we take our inquirer instead to be referring to an objective property, then the right answer might be: "It is several hundred feet tall." Another way to put this is that the formal height of the photograph (i.e., the actual height) is 7 inches whereas the objective height of the photograph (i.e., the height represented) is several hundred feet. So, a photograph needn't *be* several hundred feet tall to *represent* something that is several hundred feet tall. The analogy is instructive here. An idea needn't be extended (in length, breadth, and depth) or be shaped, for instance, in order to *represent* something that is extended or is shaped.

Descartes examines the possible *origin* of the objective reality of his ideas. Here, he introduces the distinction between *innate ideas*, *adventitious ideas*, and what are sometimes called *factitious ideas*. Innate ideas, he says, appear to have their origin in his nature (he is a finite thinking substance). His ideas of "what a thing is, what truth is, and what thought is," he says, seem "to derive from my own nature" (AT VII 38; CSM II 26). Sometimes they are cast as being *inherent* in the mind, put there by God. Adventitious ideas appear to have their origin in things existing external to (or independently of) his mind—". . . hearing a noise, as I do now, or seeing the sun, or feeling the fire, comes from things which are located outside me, or so I have hitherto judged" (*Ibid.*). Also factitious ideas appear to have their origin in the ability of the mind to put together ideas out of bits and pieces taken from the contents of other ideas.

Ideas (as a component of the epistemology)

Ideas play an additional role in Descartes's metaphysics worth mentioning. As he tells Guillaume Gibieuf, "I am certain that I can have no knowledge of what is outside me except by means of the ideas I have within me . . ." (January 19, 1642 letter to Gibieuf, AT III 474; CSMK III 201). Their additional or special role is the one they play as part of the epistemology (*epistemology* = theory of knowledge). So, not only does the metaphysics serve to tell us what there "really" is, but in Descartes's case it also provides an account of the underlying conditions for the possibility of knowledge. This sort of connection between metaphysics and epistemology was not uncommon among philosophers of the period, for it was characteristic of systems that later philosophers identified as forms of *rationalism*. Rationalism is a view (or family of views) that tells us that the possibility of knowledge of the world is found in some feature or in some set of features inherent in the mind. Since Descartes held a version of this doctrine—for example, his doctrine of innate ideas—he has been traditionally classified as a rationalist.

When focusing on his epistemology, scholars claim to find an early version of what is sometimes called "foundationalism." According to this view, Descartes establishes certain ideas (Descartes also used "proposition" in such contexts, intentionally avoiding the use of "belief." In what follows, we will stick with the term he seems to have preferred—"idea.") that served as the foundation or ground for all other ideas. They are like the axioms of Euclid's geometry, mentioned earlier. All true ideas are either directly or indirectly related to these foundational ideas. This "system" of ideas is what was earlier called a *scientia*. The "most" foundational (basic) idea for Descartes is the innate idea of God. Notice how this aligns with Descartes's metaphysical view, where God is the only true substance, and where everything else is said to depend on God for its existence (and being). This sort of connection between epistemology and metaphysics is yet another feature of Descartes's rationalism. In addition to the idea of God are the (innate) ideas of finite mind (the nature of which is to think) and indefinite body (the nature of which is to be extended). Together, they form the "foundation." The inclusion of the innate ideas of mind and body aligns (and shows the connection) with Descartes's metaphysical dualism, discussed earlier. In a letter to Princess Elisabeth, Descartes refers to the ideas of God, (finite) mind, and (indefinite) body as the *primitive notions*. They are, he says, "as it were the patterns on the basis of which we form all our other concepts" (May 21, 1643 letter to Elisabeth, AT III 665; CSMK III 218). These, he says elsewhere, are the *principles* of his philosophy (everything stems from them and can be understood ultimately in terms of them). So, God, mind, body, substance, attribute, and mode are important elements of the metaphysics—the root system of the tree.

Descartes's physics: The trunk

There were a variety of "sciences" during the period that were taken by their adherents as advancing some form of physics. Also, among them were a variety taken by their adherents as being true to the physics of Aristotle. The problem, however, is that there were a number of competing "Aristotelian" views; there was no single, coherent Aristotelian physics in the seventeenth century. Instead, it would be better to see them as forming a family of related views, some more similar than others, where we might give to this family the name "Aristotelianisms" (plural). Why is this important? It is important because Descartes is traditionally understood as reacting to *Aristotle's* physics. But, given that there was no one such physics, but a variety of "Aristotelian" physics, we might do better to take him as reacting to some version (or to some number of versions) of Aristotelian physics. It would be more accurate to say, then, that he was reacting not so much to Aristotle's physics, that is, to the physics of the *historical* Aristotle, but to the physics propounded by the various Aristotelianisms of the period.

One component of Aristotelian physics that was common to many of the Aristotelianisms in the period took the physics to be based on the qualities *hot*, *cold*, *wet*, and *dry*. The idea was that *hot* and *cold* were natural contraries, as were *wet* and *dry*. Given that nothing can possess contrary properties, nothing could be both *hot* and *cold* at the same time (in the same respect), nor could a thing be both *wet* and *dry* at the same time (in the same respect). But something could be both *hot* and *dry*, or *hot* and *wet*, or *cold* and *dry*, or *cold* and *wet*. In fact, these combinations formed the four Aristotelian natural elements: **fire** (*hot* and *dry*), **air** (*hot* and *wet*), **earth** (*cold* and *dry*), and **water** (*cold* and *wet*). Descartes tells Mersenne in a letter that in order to establish the principles of his physics he must first destroy those of Aristotle's. Here, among those principles to be "destroyed" are these qualities—hot, cold, wet, and dry. Descartes writes: "[A]nd I may tell you, between ourselves, that these six Meditations contain all the foundations of my physics. But please do not tell people, for that might make it harder for supporters of Aristotle to approve them. I hope that readers will gradually get used to my principles, and recognize their truth, before they notice that they destroy the principles of Aristotle" (January 28, 1641 letter to Mersenne, AT III 298; CSMK III 173). Descartes will base his physics on the view that the nature of material reality (i.e., body) is extension (in length, breadth, and depth), and not the sensible qualities of hot, cold, wet, and dry. His is a physics informed entirely by the nature of body, extension, where any reference made to the "properties" of bodies will be in terms of the various modes of body, which, recall, are size, shape, motion, and so on.

Descartes's plan to destroy Aristotle's principles took a rather simple, straightforward path. Descartes had some idea of the plan quite early in his career. For example, we find it in a very early work, *The World* (c. 1630s). But, we find it again in the *Meditations* (1641), and again still in later work, such as *Description of the Human Body* (c. 1647). The plan is this: to show that our ideas of hot, cold, wet, and dry are inherently problematic, and so they are utterly unreliable. If Aristotle's physics is based on such ideas, his physics rests on shaky ground. So, in *The World*, for instance, Descartes considers his sensory idea of sound. "Most philosophers," he says, "maintain that sound is nothing but a certain vibration of air which strikes our ears" (AT XI 5; CSM I 82). But his sensory idea of *sound*, that is, the idea that presents to him a certain *quality*, is not anything like the vibration of air particles. "Thus," he concludes, "if the sense of hearing transmitted to our mind the true image of its object then, instead of making us conceive the sound, it would have to make us conceive the motion of the parts of the air which is then vibrating against our ears" (*Ibid.*). The implication is straightforward: the sensory idea of the quality *sound*, assuming it is an image of the vibration of air particles, is a *false* image.

In the Third Meditation, Descartes introduces the notion of material falsity. It is a kind of falsity inherent in certain kinds of ideas—where the worry is again about his sensory ideas. An idea is materially false, he says, whenever it represents a nonexistent thing as though it were an existent thing (AT VII 43; CSM II 30). The sensory idea of cold is his example. Suppose that someone is holding an ice cube. The motions of the particles that constitute the ice cube cause certain changes in motion of the particles constituting the hand. These motions in turn are "transmitted" to the brain *via* the nerves. Even so, what arises in the mind is the sensory idea of cold. That is, the ice cube is represented as being *cold*. Like sound, cold is a quality. Like the false sensory idea of sound, the sensory idea of cold, Descartes says, is misleading. Along the lines of what he says in *The World*, were it a true image of its object, the sensory idea would represent to the mind the motions of the particles constituting the ice cube. In this case, instead of calling it a false image, he casts the idea of cold as being materially false. Although different, they are no doubt perfectly compatible notions.

Lastly, in *Description of the Human Body*, Descartes gives an account of how our sensory experience differs from what causes it. He imagines a world filled with tiny ball-like particles that are moving around. There are two motions to consider. First is the rectilinear motion of the balls as they approach the eye. Second is the motion of each ball as it turns around its own center. "If the speed at which they turn is much smaller than that of their rectilinear motion," he says, "the body from which they come appears *blue* to us; while if the turning speed is much greater than that of their rectilinear motion, the body appears *red* to us" (AT XI 256; CSM I 323). Like sound and cold, blue and red are qualities. These ideas can mislead us. They are all "false images" of their objects. So, given that Aristotle bases his entire physics on the qualities hot, cold, wet, and dry, he bases his physics on what amount to false images.

Several concepts were taken by natural philosophers of the period to be at the core of physics: the concepts of *space*, *body*, *motion*, and *time*. Thomas Hobbes, for instance, in Part II of his book *De corpore* (1655), a book that was in part a response to Descartes's *Principles*, shows how all of physics is made intelligible *via* the phantasms (i.e., ideas) of *space*, *time*, *body*, and *motion*. For Descartes, both the ideas of *space* and (individuated) *body* are derived directly from the innate idea of body (something that Hobbes rejected). This is one sense in which Descartes's physics is rooted in his metaphysics. Descartes expends a great deal of energy making out how *space* is simply a way of conceiving extension, where in terms of the metaphysics, there is no essential difference between it and *body* (again, something that Hobbes rejected). Suppose that we hold that some body *A* is surrounded by "empty space." Insofar as *A* is considered a body, something with a shape and size, it is extended by its very nature. But so is the surrounding space. In fact, space, in being essentially extended, is as much a "body" as is *A*. What "separates" the inside of *A* from the outside of *A* is *A*'s surface, where *A*'s surface is importantly related to what Descartes calls *local motion*. Both the "inside" and "outside" of A are extended. The cosmos is thus a plenum, a three-dimensional extendedness, individual bodies such as A being nothing more than carved out regions of the plenum (where the "carving" is done by way of *motion*). Descartes introduces several concepts to help make sense of the view that there are individuated bodies, such as A. For example, he introduces the concepts of *space*, *place*, *internal place*, *external place*, to name several. Each of these is simply a way of conceiving a certain region of the plenum. *Motion* for Descartes was understood as being *relative*. There was no absolute motion. So, if body A moves, it moves in relation to some other body B. This was one aspect of Descartes's physics with which Isaac Newton (1642–1727), for instance, strongly disagreed. Descartes took *rest* and *motion* to be "opposites." Also, given that there was no absolute motion, there was no absolute rest. Both were relative: a body at rest with respect to another body may be in motion with respect to yet another. Lastly, *time*, Descartes tells us, is simply a way of our conceiving the *duration* of some thing (whether in motion or at rest). In being *a way of conceiving*, time is understood as being a mode of thought. The only true properties of the bodies that inhabit the cosmos are their sizes, shapes, positions, and motions. Aristotle's *sensible qualities* (hot, cold, wet, and dry) have thus been replaced with extension and its modes.

The last important contribution that we'll consider on this front is Descartes's introduction of the concept of a *law of nature*. He suggests that the laws of nature are like "rules," which are spatiotemporal expressions of the eternal, immutable will of God. Having their origin in the *eternal* (i.e., nontemporal) and *immutable* (i.e., unchangeable) will of God guarantees both their *universality* and *necessity*. Descartes offers three laws of nature. Simply put, they are:

1 A body in state S will continue in state S unless altered by something else.

2 All bodily motion is ultimately rectilinear.

3 Two bodies that collide will alter either in trajectory or in quantity of motion.

Newton incorporated Descartes's first and second laws into his first law: "Every body continues in its state of rest, or of uniform motion in a straight line, unless it is compelled to change that state by forces impressed upon it" (Newton's *Principia* (1686), "Axioms, or Laws of Motion," Law I). What is more, the first and third laws of Descartes's system express an important component of modern physics: the idea of a *conservation* principle. Interestingly enough, Hobbes, mentioned earlier, also laid down a conservation principle about motion and rest that look very similar to Descartes's first law, but, unlike Descartes, he did not cast it as a "law" of nature. For Descartes, such a principle dictates that there are certain *quantities* of features of the cosmos, which God introduced, that remain the same over time. The *quantity of motion* is an example. Although the specific quantities of the motions of individual bodies can (and very likely will) vary over time, the *overall* quantity of motion in the cosmos will remain constant. Descartes referred to the specific quantities of individual bodies as measures of *local* motion, mentioned earlier. This was different from consideration of the overall quantity of motion. So, the local motions of bodies can change relative to one another without there being a change in the overall quantity of motion in the cosmos. As one might expect, this was considered an important conceptual advance in physics.

Medicine, mechanics, and morals: The branches

In light of the tree analogy, Descartes notes that when one sets out to pick fruit from a tree one picks from the ends of the branches (where the fruit is located)—certainly not from the roots or trunk. So, the real payoff when it comes to the system of knowledge (represented as the tree) is to be found in the sciences of medicine, mechanics, and morals. The fruit that emerges from these branches, he says, is the principal benefit of philosophy. Let's look briefly at each branch.

Medicine

In Part Six of the *Discourse* (1638), Descartes says that health is "the chief good and the foundation of all the other goods in this life" (AT VI 62; CSM I 143). Maintaining good health is one of the most important things a human being can do. Medicine is the science dedicated to the maintenance of good health. Clearly, in being a "branch," it is a science nourished by the "priori" sciences, namely the science that is analog to the "trunk" (the physics), and the science that is analog to the "roots" (the metaphysics). So, complete knowledge of medicine would require knowledge of physics and metaphysics. Descartes says toward the close of Part Six that he was prepared to dedicate the remainder of his life to a pursuit of acquiring knowledge of the "rules" (i.e., laws) that ground and ultimately structure medical science. To this end, Descartes showed a great deal of interest in anatomy and physiology. One of the earliest discussions of subject matter in this area is found in his *Treatise On Man* (c. 1629–33). This subject matter is again discussed in Part Five of the *Discourse* (1638), and again in the Sixth Meditation (1641). A work that focused specifically on anatomy and physiology was *Description of the Human Body* (1647–8). In an early letter, dated 1637, he mentions that he was working on a compendium of medicine (December 4, 1637 letter to Huygens, AT I 649; CSMK III 76). In a later letter, he says, "the preservation of health has always been the principal end of my studies . . ." (October 1645 letter to the Marquess of Newcastle, AT IV 329; CSMK III 275). So, if we take Descartes at his word, this branch meant quite a bit to him.

The concept of *life*, or of living things, was, for Descartes, clearly related to the concept of health and as a subject fell within the domain of the science of medicine. Schools in the period had adopted variations of Aristotle's model, which cast life as an emergent phenomenon of an active organizing principle in nature, the *psyche* (pronounced *puh-sookay*). The Latin translation of this Greek word was "*anima*." From this Latin word, we get such English words as "animal" and "animation." The *psyche* or *anima* is that which *animates* things—the animation expressing what it is to be a living thing. The English counterpart to *psyche* or *anima* was *soul*, a term perhaps more familiar to the reader. The *psyche* or *soul* was responsible for organizing matter where the result was a structured, self-sustaining organism. The *psyche* informed such organisms by taking matter from the surrounding environment, integrating some of what was taken into the organism, and discarding matter back into the environment. This process might be understood as a basic model of *respiration*, which might be thought to inform what are now called catabolic and anabolic processes. The most primitive level of psychic organization is what Aristotelians referred to as the *vegetative* level. All plant life is found here. But imagine that the *psyche* works to organize such things so that what emerges are more complex structures. Something new emerges: a moving, perceiving organism. This is a level of psychic organization referred to as the *animal* level. Since locomotion and perception arise at this level, it was sometimes referred to as the *perceptive* level. But imagine that the *psyche* goes to work to complicate even these new structures. A level can be reached, as in the case of the human being, where what emerges from this highly complex organized "body" is *thought* or *reason*. This was referred to as the *rational* level of psychic organization. Here, what emerges is what Aristotelians called *nous* (pronounced *noose*), or in English, *mind*. Since each of the "higher" levels of psychic organization is based on the level below it, the human being was the expression of all three levels—vegetative, perceptive, and rational.

Descartes's view of the human being can be seen as a response to the above sort of Aristotelian model. According to Descartes, the bodies of plants and animals, including those of the human being, are nothing more than complex machines, no different in principle from other machines such as clocks and fountains. "Living" things are to be completely understood in terms of applied mechanics—in terms of levers, pulleys, and so on. This eliminated the need to use Aristotle's *psyche* to explain the phenomenon called "life." Even so, Descartes did not completely abandon the use of *psyche* or *soul*. The soul, he argued, is better identified with what Aristotle had identified as the mind. So, unlike Aristotle who took the soul and mind to be different, Descartes took them to be identical. Further, again unlike Aristotle who's view looks to have entailed that the mind depends in some important sense on matter (since mind (*nous*) emerges from its organization), Descartes held, as established by his metaphysics, that mind could (and does) exist independently of matter. The human being was a *union* of mind and body, but the mind (i.e., the soul) existed utterly independently of body. Descartes is in fact among those philosophers responsible for identifying the soul with the mind.

Influence of this can be seen centuries later, when certain thinkers (e.g., Sigmund Freud, Carl Jung, William James, etc.), in working out their theories of *mind*, would call their field of study "psychology" ("psychologie" in German), the word rooted in the Greek word *psyche*.

Mechanics

Mechanics was typically taken to be a form of (applied) mathematics. Although Descartes recognized this, that mechanics "took refuge with the mathematicians" (letter to Plempius for Fromondus, October 3, 1637, AT I 421; CSMK III 64), he thought that it nevertheless should be considered a "part of the true physics" (*Ibid.*). Mechanics focuses specifically on the notion of a *machine* and on the *work* it was able to do. It is worth mentioning that Descartes did not think that machines were solely artificial (manmade) objects. "For I do not recognize any difference," he says in the *Principles*, "between artifacts and natural bodies except that the operations of artifacts are for the most part performed by mechanisms which are large enough to be easily perceivable by the senses . . ." (AT VIIIA 326; CSM I 288). So, the only real difference between manmade machines and those found in nature, as he suggests here, is that the former are typically objects that exist at the sensory level, whereas the latter, or so goes the suggestion, can be understood to be at work below the sensory level. Nature, then, might be conceived as a system of tiny machines. He goes on to say in the letter to Plempius that "mechanics is a division or special case of physics . . . [where] all the explanations belonging to the former also belong to the latter" (*Ibid.*). This can easily be understood to align with the tree analogy, since mechanics (a branch) will depend importantly on physics (the trunk). Along with a letter to Huygens (October 3, 1637), in fact, Descartes sends "three sheets" (i.e., pages), which offer some detailed discussion on machines: the pulley, the inclined plane, the wedge, the cogwheel, the screw, and the lever (AT I 434–47; CSMK III 66–73). One might even think of medicine, the previously discussed branch, as being a kind of applied mechanics (of course, thinking of it this way might violate the tree analogy, making medicine a branch of a branch, instead of taking it, as Descartes asserts, as being a branch of the trunk).

Morals

It is not always clear what constituted the science of "morals" for Descartes—this, despite the fact that he tells us on occasion what he means by it. In the very *Principles* passage in which he introduces the tree analogy, he says, "By 'morals' I understand the highest and most perfect moral system, which presupposes a complete knowledge of the other sciences and is the ultimate level of wisdom" (AT IXB 14; CSM I 186). Of course, since morals is supposed to be its own branch, distinct from medicine and mechanics, one wonders why one would *need* to know these other sciences to know anything about morals, if by the other sciences he was including medicine and mechanics. But perhaps he means to include only physics and metaphysics here. Since morals is a branch of the trunk, and the trunk is physics, then it is easy to see that moral science would be supported or underwritten by the physics, which in turn would be supported or underwritten by the metaphysics (the roots). So, in this case a complete knowledge of morals would require knowledge of physics and metaphysics. In this very same passage he goes on to remind his readers that earlier in the *Discourse* he had laid down a basic "moral code," meant to protect the reader from harm while engaged in philosophical contemplation. He had introduced his provisional moral code in Part Three. There, he offered four basic rules. First, obey the laws and customs of one's country; second, once the most probable view or action had been adopted or decided on, stick with it and do not vary; third, always aim at mastering one's self as opposed to the world (or the events outside of one's control); and fourth, choose the best occupation (of one's time), which will allow one to pursue the truth.

In the larger scheme of things, it is the *human being* conceived as the *union* of mind and body that the moral code is aimed at protecting. The ultimate harm to a human being so conceived is death, where death is the separation of mind and body, the destruction of the union. To be sure, as was noted in the section on metaphysics, Descartes held that the mind can exist independently of the body (they are really distinct), and held that post-separation from the body the mind would continue to exist. So, death is not a harm to the mind *per se*. But even at some point after death, at least if we take what he says seriously about what happens according to Catholic doctrine, Descartes says that the mind (or soul) is reunited with *a* body—according to St. Paul, this will be a "spiritual" body. Be that as it may, it is in God's creating the union, even if now after the *Fall of Man* the union is only temporary, Descartes seems to think that one has an obligation to preserve it for as long as possible.

The most sustained treatment of anything that looks like moral theory for Descartes is found in *The Passions of the Soul* (1648). Although the earlier description of Descartes's moral view makes him look like a utilitarian (or at least a consequentialist), in the *Passions* his view looks more like a version of virtue theory. It is interesting that the two look compatible—his quasi-consequentialist and quasi-virtue theory leanings—at least as he develops them. The view in the *Passions* is based on the human being conceived as the union of mind and body. Here is one place where metaphysics is presupposed in moral science. When something in the body (a motion) occasions a thought in the mind, the thought, especially if it expresses something like a desire, is called a "passion." The particular part of the body responsible for occasioning such thoughts is the pineal gland. God has instituted the union so that when the gland moves one way, it occasions a thought in the mind, and when it moves another way, it occasions yet another thought.

So, suppose that one sees the Queen and *via* natural bodily processes one is "attracted" (physically) to the Queen. The pineal gland is thus moving in such a way so as to occasion this thought (here, expressing desire for the Queen). Now, suppose that this also begins to set one's body into motion, where one's legs move, setting one on a trajectory aimed at the Queen. What are the possible consequences of approaching the Queen in this way (where the aim of the action is to satisfy one's desire for her)? Certainly, one possible consequence is that one will succeed at wooing the Queen. But, what would very likely happen were the King to discover one's affair with the Queen? No doubt heads would roll! This outcome would spell the end to one's union. One's obligation, noted earlier, is to preserve the union for as long as possible. So, if one were to allow the current desire for the Queen to continue (this is the thought occasioned by the occurring motion of the pineal gland), it might culminate in bringing an end to one's union. Now, suppose that the very thought of being beheaded quells the desire for the Queen—in other words, this thought keeps the other at bay. One literally stops in one's tracks. What has happened? On Descartes's view, one's will has summoned the idea of one's beheading, a likely outcome of successfully fulfilling the occurring desire for the Queen, and this thought has shown itself to have enough "force" to push the gland in the opposite direction, opposite to that which is occasioning the thought (expressing desire for the Queen). Here is one place where physics is presupposed in moral science. Now, it is clear in our case of the Queen that one has a choice: either continue with the thought (expressing desire for the Queen) or continue to summon the thought (expressing avoidance of beheading). Choosing the one that preserves the union is the "best" choice. Some have in fact referred to this principle—the principle that says that we are to always act on that reason (thought) that is most likely to preserve the union—as *the principle of the best*. To choose to act on this principle is, on Descartes's account, to pursue virtue (AT XI 442; CSM I 382). Our pursuing virtue is evidence of our possessing a virtuous character.

Descartes in the classroom

The *Discourse* was taught briefly at the University of Utrecht, in 1638, by one of Descartes's friends, Reneri (Henri Regnier, 1593–1639). This is probably the first time that Descartes's work was taught in the classroom. Even so, the *Discourse* would not have been something that students would have been assigned to read—students in those days were not assigned reading material as they are today. Textbooks back then were for professors, not for students. So, in line with how textbooks were used back then, what Reneri would have done was lecture from the book, using it as a guide for the course. Regius (Henri le Roy, 1598–1679), friend to both Reneri and Descartes, also taught Descartes's physics in his courses. Although this came to an abrupt end after Regius got into some trouble with university officials. The first "textbook" that Descartes explicitly intended to be used by professors in the classroom was in fact the *Meditations*. He intended it to replace a widely used textbook of the period, the *Summa philosophiae quadrapartita* (Paris, 1609), written by Eustachius à Sancto Paulo (1573–1640). Matters are complicated for the use of Descartes's work in the classroom, however, when his books were placed on the *Index*, a Catholic list of prohibited books, in 1663.

Newton discussed Descartes's views in his classes at Cambridge, on some accounts as early as the 1670s. Edmond Pourchot (1651–1734) taught Descartes's views at the University of Paris during the 1690s. Immanuel Kant (1724–1804) very likely discussed Descartes's views in the classroom. Even so, it is very likely that none of these professors required their students to read Descartes. We begin to find professors actually assigning readings by the mid-eighteenth century. For example, William Small (1734–75), professor of natural philosophy at William and Mary, assigned to his students, including the young Thomas Jefferson (1743–1826), John Locke's (1632–1704) *An Essay Concerning Human Understanding* (1690). Even though Small did not assign anything written by Descartes, assigning Locke's *Essay* would have certainly exposed his students to Descartes's views.

When Bertrand Russell (1872–1970) was a student at Cambridge, he took two history of philosophy courses during the academic year 1893–94—one from James Ward and the other from G. F. Stout. Descartes was covered in both courses. So, here it looks like Descartes's writings are actually being assigned as student reading. Russell wrote several student papers that focused on Descartes. Even so, there were few books available to students that would have included Descartes's works. There were English translations that had emerged as early as the 1650s, but they would have been rare (and expensive) during Russell's school days. The now famous *Oeuvres de Descartes*, put together by Charles Adam and Paul Tannery (referred to in this dictionary as AT), would not be published until 1897. So, Russell would not have had this collection available to him, at least not when writing these early student papers.

There are at least two books that Russell could have used in his studies of Descartes, both published in the late 1800s. There was a French volume, *Oeuvres Choisies de Descartes*, edited by Antoine Guénard (Paris: Garnier Frères, 1876), which included *Discours de la Méthode*, *Méditations Métaphysiques*, *Des Passions en Général, Règles Pour la Direction de l'Esprit*, and *Recherches Par la Lumière Naturelle*. Also, there was an English volume, *The Philosophy of Descartes: Extracts From His Writings*, translated by Henry A. P. Torrey (New York: Henry Holt & Co., 1892), which divided Descartes's philosophy into six parts: *Method*, *Metaphysics*, *Physics*, *Physiology*, *Psychology*, and *Ethics*. Torrey's division of Descartes's work into these categories aligns with the way that the academy divided philosophical systems. That Torrey orders Descartes's philosophy in this form shows that some effort had been made, though some of this was probably done prior to Torrey, to make Descartes's philosophy ready for student consumption. Extracts are taken from the *Discourse*, the *Rules*, the *Meditations*, the *Principles*, *The World*, the *Treatise on Man*, and the *Passions*. Given that Russell refers to Descartes's work with French titles, he looks to have used either the French book mentioned or some book like it.

It is perhaps no surprise that Descartes's views become subject matter for serious scholarship (in the form of papers, dissertations, books, etc.) soon after his work is being read by students. For instance, Étienne Gilson (1884–1978) would write his dissertation on Descartes, in 1913, at the University of Paris, *La Liberté chez Descartes et la Théologie* (Alcan, 1913). Martial Guéroult (1891–1979), who would take over for Gilson as professor (Collège de France) in 1951, wrote a critical study of Descartes's "system" in two volumes, *Descartes selon l'order des Raisons* (Paris, 1953). Guéroult's book would have a significant impact on future Descartes scholarship. Many in this generation (the generation of Gilson, Russell, Guéroult, etc.), but especially those who studied in England, emphasized epistemological (and downplayed metaphysical) concerns in their philosophical studies of Descartes. As a consequence, there emerged a bias as to how Descartes's views were subsequently presented and taught to students of the early and mid-twentieth century, namely as someone primarily interested in epistemology.

Out of this next generation of scholar-teacher, working and teaching in the mid- to late-twentieth century, arose new books written on Descartes's views. Although many remained convinced of the view of Descartes as arch-epistemologist, others began to see that there was much more to his views than they were originally taught. There are at least three books that would have a palpable impact on future Descartes (or "Cartesian") scholarship, especially among those studying in the United Kingdom, the United States, and Canada. The first was Richard Popkin's *The History of Scepticism from Erasmus to Descartes* (Assen: Van Gorcum, 1960). The second was Richard Watson's *The Downfall of Cartesianism* (The Hague: Martinus Nihoff, 1966). The third was Anthony Kenny's *Descartes: A Study of His Philosophy* (New York: Random House, 1968). Popkin's book was among those that focused on Descartes as being primarily an epistemologist. Watson's book introduced scholars to a host of French and Dutch philosophers: some contemporaries of Descartes, others immediately following in his wake—the "Cartesians" as they are now known. Although philosophically weighty, this book emphasized the *history* side of what we now think of as the history of philosophy. As just noted, there was a significant body of French and Dutch scholarship that Watson helped readers sort through, which offered to the English-speaking world some idea of *who* had already said *what* about Descartes. This prevented the reinvention of many a scholarly wheel, and was a great help to those coming to Descartes for the first time in their research, for sorting through this material has time and again proven itself to be a monumental hurdle to producing new research.

Like Popkin's book, Kenny's book introduced scholars to the idea that Descartes had something to offer to today's (analytic) philosopher. Although historically weighty, these books emphasized the *philosophy* side of the history of philosophy. They were able to correct some of the mistakes (both historical and philosophical) made by earlier philosophers in their respective treatments of Descartes—Russell and Ryle to name two. Another important book followed almost immediately: Harry Frankfurt's *Demons, Dreamers, and Madmen* (Indianapolis: Bobbs-Merrill, 1970). The next significant wave of books to hit (all in 1978) included Margaret Wilson's *Descartes* (London: Routledge & Kegan Paul, 1978), Edwin Curley's *Descartes Against the Skeptics* (Cambridge, MA: Harvard University Press, 1978), and Bernard Williams's *Descartes: The Project of Pure Enquiry* (New York: Penguin, 1978). It would not be an exaggeration to claim that many if not most of the Descartes scholars working today (one of whom may in fact be your teacher!), in the early twenty-first century, who earned their doctorates before the close of the twentieth century, cut their scholarly teeth (as graduate students) on one of the books mentioned earlier. Much of what is taught to undergraduates today about Descartes can very likely be traced to one or more of these books.

Terms and names

A

A posteriori/A priori. These are Latin phrases, which translated mean *from what is or comes later* (*a posteriori*) and *from what is or comes before* (*a priori*). The distinction they express has a long history in philosophy, specifically a distinction drawn between two kinds of justification, and in turn two kinds of knowledge. Let's take them one at a time, beginning with *a posteriori*.

Many students today first run across these terms when first studying Kant. He used the phrase *a posteriori* to denote a form of justification involving an appeal to sensory experience. For example, the truth of the claim "Jones is wearing a blue sweater" can be known only by way of an appeal to sensory experience—one must locate Jones and see whether or not she is wearing a blue sweater. If she is, the claim is found to be true; if she is not, the claim is found to be false. But the point is that without this observation the truth of such a claim cannot be known. This conception of justification is related to the concept of an *empirical* claim, or at least to one version of it, where a claim p is empirical if, and only if, p is falsifiable by way of sensory experience. We find some hint in Descartes's writings of the role of sensory experience and its part in justification, but nothing that would clearly relate Descartes's usage of *a posteriori* to this Kantian or post-Kantian form of justification. For example, Descartes hints at a connection in the *Discourse*. There, Descartes says of claims related to reasoning from effect to cause, which is a form of reasoning that Aquinas had referred to as *a posteriori*, that "experience" makes the former claims, those that express the effect, "quite certain" (AT VI 76; CSM I 150). The idea seems to be that supposing that we wish to pin down the cause of some given effect, where the effect is given to (or perhaps confirmed by) one's sensory experience, the form of reasoning that we would employ, using Aquinas's meaning, is *a posteriori* reasoning. So, although there is some reference to sensory experience in connection to this phrase, it is not at all clear that Descartes thought the connection essential. Rather, the phrase seems better understood in connection to the *form* of reasoning that one employs. As just noted, Aquinas used the phrase *a posteriori* to denote a form of reasoning that began with an effect and proceeded to the identifying of the cause or causes of that effect. The phrase denoted the *order* of causal elements in a proof or in an explanation, in this case from effect back to cause. But as some have noted, even though Descartes will sometimes use the phrase as did Aquinas, this is not the sense in which Descartes chooses to use the phrase in connection to his own view.

We get some idea of how Descartes uses *a posteriori* in connection to his own view by looking at his discussions of method. According to Descartes, there are two kinds of method that were available to philosophers, namely, analysis and synthesis. He specifically relates *a posteriori* to synthesis. In the Second Replies, Descartes says that synthesis is a method that begins with assumptions (premises) from which one derives specific conclusions. In light of the method of synthesis, he casts *a posteriori* reasoning as likewise moving from assumption (premise) to conclusion (AT VII 156; CSM II 110–1). In the *Discourse*, Descartes will use causal language in addition to argumentative language, where he suggests there that one employs *a posteriori* reasoning by granting the cause and deriving the effect (AT VI 76; CSM I 150). Moving from cause to effect is analogous to moving from premise to conclusion. Given that Aquinas took *a posteriori* reasoning to move from effect to cause, and yet Descartes takes it to instead move from cause to effect, Descartes clearly is not using the term as did Aquinas (in fact, Descartes seems to mean by *a posteriori* in these contexts what Aquinas meant by *a priori*). Even so, this is not because Descartes has bungled Aquinas's view. For, in a letter to Mersenne (May 10, 1632), written 5 years before publishing the *Discourse*, Descartes describes *a posteriori* reasoning along the lines of how Aquinas described it, as starting with an effect and moving to discovering its cause (AT I 251; CSMK III 38). He repeats to Plempius in another letter (December 20, 1637), the year the *Discourse* is published, that *a posteriori* reasoning moves from effect to cause (AT I 476; CSMK III 77). As we saw with the *Discourse* passage noted in the previous paragraph, he used the phrase as did Aquinas. But when he discusses the particulars of his own view, Descartes departs from Aquinas. As stressed in this entry, Descartes's departure from Aquinas appears to stem directly from his relating *a posteriori* reasoning to the method of synthesis.

Let's now address *a priori*. Again following Kant, eighteenth-century philosophers used the term *a priori* to denote a form of justification that did not require any appeal to sensory experience. Not only could the truth of an *a priori* claim be knowable independently of sensory experience, discoverable by reason alone, but it was also understood to be necessary. Kant had argued that the truths of mathematics (i.e., the truths of mathematical propositions), for example, were *a priori*. This was so because they were ultimately rooted in (or were about) space and time, conditions that are necessary for the very possibility of sensory experience, or for the very possibility of *intuition* as he called it. Kant referred to space and time as the underlying *forms* of intuition. To be sure, a mathematical proposition would be true in any and every instance of sensory experience, which is one reason why it was taken to be necessary (and universal), but it wasn't true because of anything specific to any *instance* of sensory experience. A mathematical proposition is true in any and every instance of sensory experience precisely because its truth is rooted in (or is about) the *forms* of sensory experience (space and time), in the very conditions that make sensory experience or intuition even possible. Descartes does not ever clearly make the connection between the phrase *a priori* and this Kantian or post-Kantian form of justification. Even so, he does recognize our having a kind of knowledge that is not related to sensory experience. In a letter to Voetius, published in May 1643, he claims that some truths can be known "without any sensory experience" (AT VIIIB 166–7; CSMK III 222). "All geometrical truths," he says, "are of this sort . . ." (*Ibid.*). Be that as it may, as with *a posteriori*, Descartes associates *a priori* with a certain kind of method, namely with analysis. (Recall that he related *a posteriori* to the method of synthesis.) "Analysis," he says in the Second Replies, "shows the true way by means of which the thing in question was discovered methodically and as it were *a priori*, so that if the reader is willing to follow it and give sufficient attention to all points, he will make the thing his own and understand it just as perfectly as if he had discovered it for himself" (AT VII 155; CSM II 110).

Aquinas had used the phrase *a priori* to denote a form of reasoning that began with a cause and proceeded to the identifying of the effect of that cause. So, the phrase denoted the *order* of causal elements in the proof or explanation. In argumentative terms, this form of reasoning began with an assumption (or premise) and then sought the conclusion that followed. More on this shortly. As with *a posteriori*, in letters written before the publishing of the *Meditations*, Descartes employs *a priori* along the lines of Aquinas (e.g., in a letter to Mersenne, May 10, 1632: AT I 250–1; CSMK III 38). However, as some have noted, there are places, for example, in the Second Replies passages quoted in the previous paragraph, where Descartes will stray from Aquinas's use of the phrase (CSM II 110, fn. 2). As quoted at the close of the previous paragraph, Descartes does more than to suggest that the phrase is importantly connected to a form of reasoning associated with the method of analysis, in which one begins with an effect and then seeks to discover its cause. We again find this way of depicting analysis in the Fourth Replies (AT VII 155; CSM II 110). In argumentative terms, recall, Aquinas held that *a priori* reasoning begins with a premise (here analog to a given cause) and then seeks to discover the conclusion (here analog to an effect) that follows.

When discussing method and the various forms of reasoning, it is not clear that Descartes is concerned solely with justification, for in some cases he seems interested in providing instead what might be better taken as an explanation. For, he did see a difference between justification, proof, and explanation (letter to Morin, July 13, 1638: AT II 198; CSMK III 106). Rather, the following seems closer to what he had in mind. Consider, for example, our perceiving some object *s*. Let's say that we see that *s* is shaped. Let this perception be our starting point (even so, in this context our "starting point" will be analog to an effect or a conclusion). What Descartes discovers by way of analysis is that *s*'s being extended is a necessary condition for *s*'s being shaped. If *s* was not extended, *s* could not be shaped. This discovery of the relation between "*s* is shaped" and "*s* is extended"

(Descartes will more often speak of these as being *ideas*; so the idea that exhibits *s as shaped* and the idea that exhibits *s as extended*) was not accomplished by way of an empirical inquiry. Rather, it was "perceived by the mind alone" and was established by way of a "purely mental scrutiny" (AT VII 31; CSM II 21). As he later would put the relation between these two things in the *Principles*, "shape is unintelligible except in an extended thing" (AT VIIIA 25; CSM I 210). So, what we discover is that what underwrites the very possibility of *s*'s being shaped is *s*'s being extended. Descartes's sense of *a priori* seems to apply here: we could not even conceive *s* as being shaped without also conceiving *s* as being extended. There is a sense, then, in which the claim "*s* is extended," or the idea that exhibits *s as extended*, is shown to be necessary (given "*s* is shaped" or given the idea that exhibits *s as shaped*), and a sense in which it is discovered to be so independently of sensory experience. Here, in noting that "*s* is extended" is necessary, we might say that its being extended is a necessary condition for being its shaped. Given "*s* is shaped" or given the idea that exhibits *s as shaped*, "*s* is extended" or the idea that exhibits *s as extended* is said to be *a priori*. Descartes's sense of *a priori*, then, seems to involve one's discovery of the underlying conditions that account for a thing's possibility (see, e.g., what he says to Mersenne in a letter dated October 28, 1640: AT III 212; CSMK III 154). So, whereas Aquinas held that *a priori* reasoning moves from cause to effect (or from premise to conclusion), Descartes says that it moves from effect back to cause (or from conclusion back to premise). Descartes's departure from Aquinas appears to stem directly from his relating *a priori* reasoning to the method of analysis.

Abstract/Abstraction/Exclusion (L. *abstrahendo* (v)/ *abstractionem*; F. *abstraction/exclusion*). Following along the lines of his Scholastic predecessors, Descartes takes abstraction to be an intellectual *activity* (AT X 441, 446, 449; CSM I 58, 61, 63, AT VII 117, 120, 216; CSM II 83–4, 85–6, 156, AT IXA 216; CSM II 276–7, AT III 421, 474; CSMK III 188, 201–2, AT IV 120; CSMK III 236). The concept of abstraction can be traced to Aristotle (see, e.g., *Physics* B2, 193b 23–194a 12). Descartes sometimes contrasts abstraction to what he calls *exclusion*. This entry will look at both, treating them as forming a single distinction. Let's first look at abstraction.

The mental act of abstracting is performed by the mind when it focuses on at least one ideational element in a given idea, separating it from all other ideational elements also present in the given idea. The Latin term is telling: *abstrahere* means *to drag away* or *to estrange*. For example, given the idea of the sun, we can focus on the sun's shape as represented in the idea, one of the ideational elements present in the idea of the sun, while at the same time ignoring whatever other ideational elements may be present—such as the elements representing size, color, heat, extendedness, and so on. By focusing on the ideational element *shape*, that is, by isolating it or separating it in thought from the other ideational elements, we are engaged in the intellectual act of abstracting. By way of this mental act we produce a new idea—in the case just considered, we produce the idea of a shape.

As noted earlier, Descartes contrasts exclusion and abstraction, though strictly speaking they are not opposites or contraries (AT VII 220–30; CSM II 155–61, AT IXA 215–6; CSM II 276–7, AT IV 120; CSMK III 236). Exclusion is an intellectual activity. Like abstraction, the mental act of excluding is performed by the mind when it focuses on at least one ideational element in a given idea, separating from it all other ideational elements also present in the given idea. But exclusion requires something more than abstraction, namely, the isolated ideational feature must be conceivable completely and independently of all other ideational features, specifically those features originally present in the given idea. This is shown, he suggests, by our being able to "negate" these features while nevertheless actively conceiving the isolated feature (AT IXA 215; CSM II 276). So, the ways in which one "separates" the ideational features by way of the acts of abstraction and exclusion are different. For the former, when focusing on some ideational element *s*, the separation is done by *ignoring* ideational elements other than *s*, and for the latter, the separation is done by *negating* (or completely *removing*) the ideational elements other than *s*.

In an Appendix to the Fifth Set of Objections and Replies, Descartes draws the difference between exclusion (Descartes in fact uses the French word *exclusion*) and abstraction, but also uses the Latin terms *distinguere* (to distinguish: to mark off or to divide) and *abstrahere* (to abstract: to drag away or to estrange)

(AT IXA 216; CSM II 276), where in this context the former looks to be an alternative term for *exclusion*. This distinction is repeated in a May 2, 1644 letter (presumably to Mesland), but there Descartes uses the French terms *l'exclusion* and *l'abstraction* (AT IV 120; CSMK III 236). Consider the idea of the sun. Descartes says that we can abstract shape from this idea by focusing on (i.e., isolating or separating in thought) the shape as presented in the idea and ignoring all other ideational features present in the idea of the sun, such as its color, heat, motion, position, extendedness, and so on. Even so, Descartes is clear to tell us that we cannot *exclude* extendedness, for example, from shape, for to exclude extension (the sun's length, breadth, and depth, which it possesses essentially in virtue of its being a body) would render the sun's shape unintelligible. This is so because everything that can be attributed to a body, including shape, "presupposes extension" (AT VIIIA 25; CSM I 210). That is, anything that is shaped is extended. If something were not extended, it *could not be* shaped. A non-extended shaped thing is a contradiction. Thus, although we can abstract (generally speaking) shape, we cannot exclude the ideational element *shape* from our idea of *extension*, or vice versa (given that both ideational elements are included in our idea of the sun).

Can any of our ideas or ideational elements be excluded from one another? Yes. Consider the idea of the human being, which represents the human being as a rational, corporeal being. According to Descartes we can not only abstract thinking or thought from extension—so we focus on thought while ignoring extension—but also go further and *exclude* these two ideational elements from one another. In other words, we can completely isolate our idea of mind, which includes principally in its content the ideational element *thought* or *thinking*, the *essence* of mind, from our idea of body, which includes principally in its content the ideational element *extension*, the *essence* of body, the "isolation" done by our "negating" the latter elements (AT VIIIA 25; CSM I 210). Descartes's point is that in such a case we can completely conceive mind (its nature) independently of our conceiving body (its nature), and vice versa. Such an instance of exclusion is importantly related to what Descartes calls *real distinction* or a distinction in reality (AT VIIIA 28–9; CSM I 213. For more, see the entry for **Distinction**, **Real**). Modes of the two kinds of substance, mind and body, can also be excluded from one another. For example the idea of doubting, which is an idea of a mode of thinking, can be excluded from the idea of shape, which is an idea of a mode of extension (see what Descartes says concerning *modal distinction*: AT VIIIA 29; CSM I 213. For more, see the entry for **Distinction, Modal**). However, a possible difficulty emerges in the case of color (for color, a mode associated with thought does not appear to be conceivable independently of extendedness). This difficulty aside, Descartes says that this sort of distinction, the distinction between modes of the two kinds of substance, mind and body, might be better understood as a real distinction. Secondary Sources: Nolan (1997a, 1997b).

Act/Action (L. *actus/actionem*; F. *actes/action*). These terms very likely entered Descartes's philosophical vocabulary in his studies at the Jesuit college of La Flèche. They are technical terms in Scholastic philosophy, related to the Aristotelian distinctions *active–passive* and *actuality–potentiality*. In his reply to Thomas Hobbes, author of the Third Set of Objections, Descartes adopts a commonly held general metaphysical framework in which the term *act* operates. "[I]n general," Descartes says, "no act or accident can exist without a substance for it to belong to" (AT VII 176; CSM II 124). Here, an act is cast as a property that depends ontologically on some substance. This ontological claim finds support in Descartes's epistemological view that a substance cannot be known in itself, that is, as something completely isolated from its properties (for Descartes, the latter are attributes or modes), but can be known "only through its being the subject of certain acts" (*Ibid.*). Specific to Descartes's dualism, now focusing on what he will in the *Principles* call a substance's *principal attribute* (AT VIIIA 25; CSM I 210), "a thought cannot exist without a thing that is thinking" (AT VII 175; CSM II 124). A thought is an act and it belongs to a substance, the thing that has the thought. Acts of thought, he says, include understanding, willing, imagining, and sensing. The substance in which such acts inhere, Descartes says, we call *mind* (*Ibid.*). Likewise, "there are certain acts that we call 'corporeal,' such as size, shape, motion and all others that cannot be thought of apart from local extension; and we use the term 'body' to refer to the substance in which they inhere" (*Ibid.*). In this context, acts are identified as *attributes* or *modes*, both constituting an important part of Descartes's ontology (for more see the entries for **Attribute**; **Mode**; **Reality**, **Formal**; and **Distinction**, **Real**).

In a May 1641 letter to the Dutch physician Henricus Regius (1598–1679), Descartes emphasizes a distinction that he had drawn in the Sixth Meditation, which complicates the picture. He writes that willing and understanding, the two basic faculties or capacities of a mind, "differ only as the activity and passivity of one and the same substance" (AT III 372; CSMK III 182). Understanding, he says, "is the passivity of the mind," whereas "willing is its activity" (*Ibid.*). As was noted in the previous paragraph, Descartes counts the understanding among the acts of thought. So, there arises some tension with respect to his casting the understanding as an *act* of the mind and yet as a *passive* faculty or capacity. In this context the understanding appears to be cast as a *passive act* of the mind, which, if so, appears to be oxymoronic. But, there is a possible alternative. Return to the Third Replies. There, Descartes reminds Hobbes that ". . . 'thought' is sometimes taken to refer to the act, sometimes to the faculty, and sometimes to the thing which possesses the faculty" (AT VII 174; CSM II 123). The same, it would seem, would hold for *understanding*, where it can refer to an act, a faculty, or to the thing possessing the faculty. Thus, when casting the understanding as passive, Descartes can be read as not using *understanding* to denote an act but rather to denote a faculty. Thus, he need not be saddled with holding the oxymoronic *passive act*.

In other discussions of act and faculty or capacity, Descartes makes reference to the Aristotelian *actuality–potentiality* distinction. In a October 5, 1637 letter to Mersenne, for example, Descartes makes the reference, in part prompted by a critic of his *Optics* (the critic was the mathematician Pierre de Fermat). According to Descartes, his critic had argued that the tendency to move and a particular movement should be governed by distinct kinds of laws, since the tendency stands to a particular movement as potentiality stands to actuality (AT I 450; CSMK III 73–4). An assumption lurking in his critic's line of reasoning is that given that potentiality and actuality are importantly distinct ontological states of being, any laws that govern or determine them must be importantly distinct. Descartes recalls his having claimed in the *Optics* that "the tendency to move must follow in this respect the same laws as does the movement itself" (AT I 450; CSMK III 74—he cites the *Optics*, AT

VI 89; CSM I 155). In support of this claim, he says, if there exists an instance of motion, that is, an *actual* motion, there exists the potential or possibility for motion, but not the other way around—if the potential for motion exists it does not follow that there is any instance of motion, or any actual motion (AT I 451; CSMK III 74). Actuality presupposes potentiality or possibility. This logical or conceptual relation between an actual motion and the tendency or potential for motion entails that the same laws that govern the former govern the latter. This suggests that an act is to a faculty or capacity, whether mental or corporeal, as an actual motion is to the potential (i.e., power or capacity) for motion. This aligns with his remarks to Hobbes and to Regius, considered earlier.

In a July 13, 1638 letter to Jean-Baptiste Morin, Descartes notes that the term *action* is ambiguous, and "comprises not only the power or inclination to move but also the movement itself" (AT II 204; CSMK III 109). Descartes says that whenever he used the term, at least in the *Optics*, he intended it in the latter sense, to denote an instance of motion, or an actual motion (*Ibid.*), which, as was noted earlier, is what in other contexts he will refer to as an *act* of a body (i.e., a corporeal act). He again says to Morin in a follow-up letter (September 12, 1638) that the term *action* is ambiguous and can denote not only a particular act but also the tendency or inclination to move, though he again suggests that the latter is not how he is using the term (AT II 363; CSMK III 120). Thus, in discussions about motion, *act* and *action* are used by Descartes to denote actual instances of motion. The general philosophical picture suggested is that *act* and *action* work within Descartes's ontology to denote actual instances of attributes or modes of substances, regardless of whether the substance is a body (an extended thing) or a mind (a thinking thing). Thus, a particular instance of extension, such as a motion or a shape, is an act of a body, and a particular instance of thought, such as an idea or a judgment, is an act of a mind.

Action is also an important term for Descartes when discussing the nature of human beings. In Part Two of the *Principles*, Descartes mentions what he takes to be a common view of action: "we take *action* (*actionem*) to be the effort we expend in moving our limbs and moving other bodies by the use of our limbs" (AT VIIIA 54; CSM I 234). In the *Passions*, Descartes is clear to say that an action of the mind originates in the *will*; the understanding or the intellect, as was noted earlier, remains cast as a passive faculty, the capacity a mind possesses in virtue of which it can be affected. He refers to the latter as the mind's (or the soul's) *passions* (AT XI 342; CSM I 335. For more see **Passions**). There appears, then, to be at least two "agents" that can affect the mind's intellectual faculty: one's body and one's will. When the former acts on the intellect, instances of sensation (whether inner or outer) or instances of imagination arise; when the latter acts on the intellect, instances of abstract intellectual thought (e.g., when engaged in doing mathematics) or even instances of imagination arise. When a thought is brought about and maintained over some period of time by way of actions of the body, where this thought predisposes one to behave in certain ways, Descartes refers to this thought as a *passion*. In many cases, the will can counteract and suppress or oppose such a thought by willing the intellect to produce certain representations (ideas) that in turn keep the pineal gland at bay, thus neutralizing the predisposition to behave in certain ways (e.g., see AT XI 362–4, 407, 428–9; CSM I 344–5, 365, 375–6). It is by way of the pineal gland and the animal spirits that the will can act so as to move one's body (e.g., one's limbs), the intellect typically representing the motives and reasons for action (AT XI 361; CSM I 344. For more, see **Will** and **Intellect**, and **Understanding**). Those actions related to thought, regardless of whether that thought is brought about by the body or by the will, are considered to be genuinely *human* actions, and are subject to moral scrutiny and assessment (for more on this topic, see **Passions**).

Analysis/Synthesis (L. *analyticus/synthetico*; F. *analytique/synthese*). These terms refer to two kinds of method. The classical source depicting these methods is found in Pappus of Alexandria's (290 CE–350 CE) *Mathematical Collections*. Pappus's descriptions of analysis and synthesis look similar to the two methods of inquiry introduced by Socrates at the close of Book VI of Plato's *Republic*, where Socrates discusses the analogy of the divided line (*Republic*, 509d–511e). Let's take them one at a time, beginning with *analysis*.

Pappus tells us of two kinds of analysis: *theoretical* and *problematical*. Scholars have identified problematical analysis as that kind which most closely aligns to the method adopted by Descartes.

Roughly, analysis in this sense would begin with some "given," specifically some proposition or idea, and would work toward the discovery of what other proposition or idea underwrites it, where this would continue until one reached a "first principle." A first principle would be self-evidently the case, and would require nothing other than itself to account for its being the case. Thus, in causal terms, this mode of presentation begins with what would be taken to be an effect and then would work backward, so to speak, in search of the cause or causes that underwrite it (or bring it about), the analysis terminating in a first principle. In this case, the latter would be self-evidently the case. In argumentative terms, this sort of analysis would begin with what would be taken to be a conclusion and then would work toward the discovery of the premise or premises that underwrite it (or justify it), the analysis terminating in a first principle. In this case, the latter would be self-evidently true, and would require no other proposition or idea other than itself to justify its being true. Generally, then, the idea is that one begins with something assumed or hypothesized, a given, and then seeks the conditions that underlie the very possibility of the thing assumed or hypothesized, these underlying conditions ultimately revealing some first principle. This is the version of analysis that Descartes seems to have adopted. For example, in the Fourth Replies, Descartes suggests that analysis allows him to consider certain hypotheses, as though they were true or as though they were the case, and then to work toward the discovery of what *must* be true or what *must* be the case, where the latter would be what accounts for the very possibility of the things hypothesized (AT VII 248–9; CSM II 173).

Here is an example of what Descartes seems to have in mind. Suppose that we were given the Pythagorean Theorem. Analysis begins with this and then works toward a discovery of what geometrical propositions must be in play in order to account for the very possibility of the Pythagorean Theorem. Ultimately, the analysis would terminate in a discovery of the axioms (self-evident propositions) that underwrite the Pythagorean Theorem, which make the theorem possible. The axioms would be examples of first principles. In light of the *Meditations*, Descartes considers, for example, his ordinary beliefs that have their origin in the senses, and seeks out the underlying conditions that account for the very possibility of having such beliefs. In this way, the analytic method can be understood as having paved the way for his metaphysics.

The term *synthesis* denotes a type of method that ideally guides one from self-evident propositions to specific conclusions that follow (logically). As Descartes puts it in the Second Replies: "It [synthesis] demonstrates the conclusion clearly and employs a long series of definitions, postulates, axioms, theorems and problems, so that if anyone denies one of the conclusions it can be shown at once that it is contained in what has gone before, and hence the reader, however argumentative or stubborn he may be, is compelled to give his assent . . . It was synthesis alone that the ancient geometers usually employed in their writings" (AT VII 158–9; CSM II 111). Prompted by a critic, Descartes offers a brief working out of the *Meditations* in synthetic form, where he begins with definitions, moves to formulating postulates, then axioms, and then ends with deriving specific propositions (AT VII 160–70; CSM II 113–20). Here is an example of what Descartes seems to have had in mind. Suppose that we were given Euclid's definitions, postulates, and axioms. Synthesis would be the derivation of, say, the Pythagorean Theorem. Ideally, we could go further, where were we to introduce a right triangle whose hypotenuse was unknown, but whose two sides measured 3 and 4, respectively, the method of synthesis could continue, allowing us to derive the specific geometrical proposition: "The hypotenuse of the given triangle measures 5." In causal terms, synthesis would begin with a cause and then work toward the discovery of what effect must follow. Here, "cause" is analog to "premise," and "effect" is analog to "conclusion." Secondary Sources: Curley (1986) and Smith (2010b).

Animal (L. *animalibus, brutis*; F. *animal, bestes*). The French (and subsequently the English) word *animal* is derived from the Latin *anima*, the latter used in the Schools to denote the *soul*. *Anima* was the Latin translation of the Greek $\psi \upsilon \kappa \eta$ (*psyche*). According to Aristotelian philosophy, living things such as plants, animals, including human beings, were things animated by the soul (the word *animated* is also derived from the Latin *anima*). *Anima* was typically understood to be an organizing principle of matter, which accounted for the unique feature found in certain bodies known as *life*; it is what accounted for a body's being a *living* body (for more, see **Soul**).

In his Latin writings, Descartes uses *anima* to denote the *soul*. But unlike his contemporaries, he took the soul to be coextensive with the *mind*. In denying minds to animals, he also denied souls to them. In his accounts of "living" bodies, Descartes in fact abandons talk of the vegetative and sensitive levels of psychic organization, both part of the then standard Aristotelian explanation of life. Plants and animals, including the human body, are simply machines, no different in principle from well-made clocks (AT VI 56, AT VII 57; CSM I 139–40, CSM II 140, also see AT XI 202, AT VI 46; CSM I 108, CSM I 134). Perhaps as a way to avoid the connection to *anima* or soul, in his Latin writings Descartes refers to animals as *brutes* (the Latin word is *brutis*). Only on rare occasion does he use any Latin derivative of *anima* to refer to animals (e.g., at AT VII 426 he uses *animalibus*), and this is usually within the context of a reply to a critic who had used the term. In his French writings, Descartes will use *animal* and sometimes *bestes* (beasts). When specifically pressed about the Aristotelian view of psychic organization, Descartes again avoids the derivatives of *anima* when referring to animals and uses the Latin phrase *animas brutorum* (AT VII 229), which translated means "the souls of the brutes." But again, he does not take the "soul" of the animal to be anything like the *mind* of a human being, but rather casts "the souls of brutes" as certain configurations of matter, certain material structures, that dispose animal bodies to move—to breathe, to eat, to digest food, to walk, to cry out, and so on. He even says in what appears to be an attempt to placate his critics, if push came to shove, that he could see how one might want to cast such a configuration as a *corporeal soul* (see, e.g., the February 5, 1649 letter to Henry More, AT V 276; CSMK III 365). But this is not a phrase that he prefers. For Descartes, animals are complex machines—period. Since they lack souls (minds), they cannot sense, feel, reflect, opine, reason, or in short, think. Their movements are to be explained completely in terms of mechanics.

Animal Spirits (L. *spiritus animales*; F. *espritis animaux*). These are very small particles of matter that Descartes claimed can (and typically do) move very fast; so fine in fact that a collection of such particles can appear to the naked eye to be a kind of vapor. Descartes believed animal spirits to be present in the blood, and also in the nerves (which he took to be small tubes) and in the interior cavity of the brain, the latter housing the pineal gland. Like a kind of hydraulic fluid under pressure in a system, they serve as a medium in communicating motion between the brain (specifically the pineal gland), muscles, and organs (AT XI 129–32, AT VI 53–8, AT VII 230, AT VIIIA 317, AT XI 332; CSM I 100–1, CSM I 138–41, CSM II 161, CSM I 280–1, CSM I 330). The idea of *spirits* in this sense (as fine physical substances capable of moving the human body) is still echoed today, for example in advertisements of local *wine and spirits* shops, where *spirits* refers to the "spirit" known today as alcohol. Ammonia was thought to be another type of spirit. Think of how just smelling it causes one's eyes to open and one's head to jolt back. In terms of Descartes's view this might be understood as follows: the fine vapor or spirit penetrates the nasal cavity and causes a change in motion of the animal spirits present in the interior cavity of the brain, which in turn moves the pineal gland. The movement of the gland results in the opening of the eyes and the jolting back of the head.

Aquinas, Thomas (1225–74). In Descartes's day, Aquinas would have been known as *Saint* Thomas Aquinas. Among other things, Aquinas is known (philosophically) for having integrated Aristotle into Catholic theology. In a letter to Mersenne, Descartes says that he has with him a copy of the Bible and a copy of "a *Summa* of St Thomas" (December 25, 1639, AT II 630; CSMK III 142). Also, about a year later, he says to Mersenne that with respect to the Trinity, "I share St Thomas' opinion that it is a sheer article of faith and cannot be known by the natural light" (December 31, 1640, AT III 274; CSMK III 166). In the First Set of Replies, appended to the *Meditations*, Descartes again refers to Aquinas as St. Thomas (AT VII 106, 114; CSM II 77, 82) and, as is evident from the previously cited letters, shows more than just a little familiarity with Aquinas's *Summa Theologiae* (AT VII 114–5; CSM II 82). Secondary Source: McInerny and O'Callaghan (2013).

Arnauld, Antoine (1612–94). Arnauld authored the Fourth Set of Objections, appended to the *Meditations*. Among other things, he is famous for having introduced in the Fourth Objections what is now referred to as the "Cartesian Circle." In the *Meditations*, Descartes had established the "truth-rule" in connection to his clearly and distinctly perceiving something. "Whatever I perceive very clearly and distinctly is true" (AT VII 35; CSM II 24). He went on to use this rule to prove that God exists and is no deceiver. The trouble, however, as Arnauld saw it, was that the guarantee of the truth-rule was possible only *after* it was established that God exists and is no deceiver. But, the latter cannot be established without the guarantee of the truth-rule (AT VII 214; CSM II 150). In a letter to Mersenne, Descartes says that of all the Objections, Arnauld's was, in his opinion, the best (AT III 331; CSMK III 175). Arnauld would have been about 28 years old when he wrote the Fourth Objections. Not only would he continue to correspond with Descartes, but also later would correspond with two other important philosophers of the period, Malebranche and Leibniz. Among those works relevant to Descartes's views, he coauthored (with Pierre Nicole) the *La logique ou l'Art de penser* (*The Logic and the Art of Thinking*: 1662) and authored *Des varaies et des fausses idées* (*On True and False Ideas*: 1683). Secondary Sources: Newman and Nelson (1999), Lennon (2008), and Kremer (2012).

Atom (L. *atomi*; F. *atomes*). This term has its origin in ancient Greek philosophy, where τόμος (*tomos*) means *divisible* and the added α functions as a negative prefix—thus, ἄτομος (*atomos*) means *indivisible*. Descartes refers to atoms as "pieces of matter that are by their very nature indivisible" (AT VIIIA 51; CSM I 231). He argues that defined as such atoms are impossible. They are impossible since all bodies, regardless of how small they may be, are extended (in length, breadth, and depth); and anything that is extended can be divided. The division here need not be an *actual* division. For, supposing that a piece of matter was too small for anyone or anything to divide (this simply would be a practical or physical limitation), at the very least one could *conceive* the division (*Ibid.*). This is sufficient to serve as counterexample to the claim that a piece of extended matter was indivisible, where the counterexample serves to challenge the modal import of the term *indivisible*; or to put it slightly differently, it challenges the import of the modal expression "division is *impossible*." In a September 30, 1640 letter to Mersenne, Descartes notes that the term *atom* is a contradiction, the term denoting "that of being a body and being indivisible" (AT III 191; CSMK III 154). In a

January 19, 1642 letter to Guillaume Gibieuf (1591–1650), Descartes repeats that the term *atom* is a contradiction (AT III 477; CSMK III 202). Also, in a February 5, 1649 letter to Henry More (1614–87), Descartes again claims that *atom* is a contradiction, since it denotes something that is "conceived as extended and at the same time indivisible" (AT V 273; CSMK III 363). Descartes's denial of the existence of atoms is based on the idea that the very nature of body is to be extended, and that extension is divisible by its very nature. His position on the impossibility of atoms is importantly related to his denial of the existence of a vacuum (for more, see **Vacuum**).

Even so, Descartes held that there were three basic "levels" of body that some took to be consistent with versions of "atomism," although again Descartes made it a point to steer clear from any connection to the latter view. On Descartes's view, these three levels of body constituted the bodies we ultimately perceive. The third level, he says, includes the relatively larger, clunky, bulky particles, of various shapes (AT VIIIA 105; CSM I 258). The second level includes relatively smaller particles, invisible to the naked eye, which are spherical in shape. At this level, the particles (or corpuscles) move much more easily among one another than at the third level, primarily because of their spherical shapes. Even so, these second level particles can smash one another into smaller fragments (*Ibid.*). The debris of these fragments forms the first level of body. These bodies move so fast and so violently that they continue to smash one another into indefinitely smaller and smaller fragments (*Ibid.*). Be that as it may, no body, not even those at the first level, are strictly speaking "atoms," for any and every body at this level is in principle divisible into yet smaller bodies.

It is worth noting that some followers of Descartes's philosophical system did not agree with his view on the impossibility of atoms. Geraud de Cordemoy (1626–84), for instance, adopted Descartes's view that the nature of body was to be extended (in length, breadth, and depth), but in holding that body was a substance, and so incorruptible, held that there was a "level" of body, certainly below the level of perception, at which body could not be divided. This view assumes that divisibility and corruptibility are internally related, so that if something was divisible it was corruptible, and vice versa. Since body was a genuine substance, and substances cannot be corrupted (i.e., taken out of existence) by natural means anyway (God could annihilate a substance by withholding his concurrence), body cannot be divided. Hence, body is indivisible. Since the bodies we perceive can be divided, they are simply composite bodies, composed ultimately of some smallest possible bodies, that latter being indivisible. The early modern atomist Walter Charleton (1619–1707) held a similar view. According to such views, the notion of divisibility is understood in terms of *body* and *inanity* (inanity = *space* or *void*). Body A is *divisible* if, and only if, A is composed of at least two bodies B and C, where the latter are separated by inanity. As it turns out, this kind of atomism is consistent with the view of the material universe being a single *plenum*, a view that Spinoza and others would draw from Descartes's position of body as an extended substance. Secondary Sources: Ablondi (2010) and Slowik (2013).

Attribute (L. *attributa*; F. *attribut*). This is one of several technical terms that emerge in Descartes's philosophical system. In its usage that is closest to that found in Scholastic philosophy, *attribute* looks to be coextensive with *quality* or *mode* (AT VIIIA 8, 26; CSM I 196, 211). Descartes, however, importantly modifies this. The modified sense is rooted in the idea that an attribute is the most general aspect of a substance in terms of which the substance is conceived. Descartes writes: "A substance may indeed be known through any attribute at all . . ." (AT VIIIA 25; CSM I 210). An attribute also can be discovered by way of an analysis of ideas of modes or modifications. When considering various modes of a substance (*via* various ideas) the attribute is that which "remains unmodified" in one's consideration (AT VIIIA 26; CSM I 211). Here, he is not denying that the attribute is modified. Modes are modifications of attributes. So, for example, shape is a mode or modification of extension, where extension is the attribute. Rather, *unmodified* in this context refers to that which does not change when conceiving or considering various modes. Consider a finite body. Suppose that we consider it to be in motion, to have a specific shape, size, and so on. In considering its motion, shape, size, and so on, we are considering its various modes or modifications. Conceptually speaking, as was just noted about shape, such modes are modes or modifications of extension (in length, breadth, and depth). This is shown by the fact that when conceiving any of them, we necessarily conceive extension. For instance, when conceiving a finite body's shape we *ipso facto* conceive its extension (whether we are immediately aware of this or not). Shape, Descartes claims, "presupposes" (*præsupponit*) extension. In fact, "shape is unintelligible except in an extended thing" (AT VIIIA 25; CSM I 210). When considering the various modes of a body—motion, shape, and so on—what remains unmodified in our consideration is extension. That is, although motion is distinct from shape, and shape from size, and so on, the extension that is presupposed in our conceiving its motion, for instance, is also presupposed in our conceiving its shape. It is what these modes have in common. They all presuppose extension. In this sense, extension is what remains unchanged or unmodified in our considerations. In this way, one can discover that extension is an attribute.

It is not clear how many attributes are allowed in Descartes's philosophical system. In connection to his dualism, Descartes claims that there are exactly two kinds of substance in the cosmos: *thinking* and *extended* substances, or *mind* and *body*. "[E]ach [kind of] substance has one principal property which constitutes its nature and essence, and to which all its other properties refer" (AT VIIIA 25; CSM I 210). So, each kind of (finite) substance, of which there are exactly two, has what Descartes calls its *principal attribute*. Thought is the principal attribute of mind, and extension is the principal attribute of body (*Ibid.*). But there is an important relation holding between a substance and its attributes and between the attributes of the same substance, which suggests that there are more attributes than thought and extension. Descartes writes: "since a substance cannot cease to endure without also ceasing to be, the distinction between the substance and its duration is merely a conceptual one" (AT VIIIA 30; CSM I 214). What this means is that one cannot completely conceive the substance independently of the attribute through which one conceives the substance (for more, see **Distinction, Rational**). This also holds between attributes of the same substance. Thus, the distinctions between a body's extension and its duration (its existence over time), which here are counted as two attributes of body, are only conceptually or rationally distinct. We cannot conceive a body's extension independently of its duration (its existence over time), that is, in complete isolation of its duration (for more, see **Abstract/Abstraction/Exclusion** and **Distinction, Rational**). Arguably, Descartes provides a short list of "the most general terms" that denote attributes: *substance, duration, order,* and *number*. To this list he adds *thought* and *extension* (AT VIIIA 22–3; CSM I 208). Spinoza (1632–77), for instance, would interpret Descartes's system as allowing the list of attributes to be infinite, at least with respect to God (*Ethics*, translated and edited by Edwin Curley, New York: Penguin Books, 1996, Part One, definitions D4 and D6). Secondary Sources: Nolan (1997a, 1997b).

Augustine, Aurelius (354–430 CE). In Descartes's day, Augustine would have been known as *Saint* Augustine. Among other things, Augustine is known (philosophically) for having integrated Plato (and Neo-Platonism) into Catholic theology. Some of Descartes's contemporaries noted that important elements of Descartes's philosophy look to be rooted in, or even borrowed from, Augustine's writings. In response to a correspondent, Colvius, for instance, Descartes admits that his "I am thinking, therefore I exist," which appeared in his *Discourse*, could be found earlier asserted by Augustine (letter to Colvius, November 14, 1640, AT III 247–8; CSMK III 159). What is implied in this letter, however, in which Descartes expresses surprise in finding this phrase in Augustine's writings (after Colvius brought it to his attention), is that when he wrote it, he was unaware of Augustine's having said it. Arnauld, in the Fourth Set of Objections, also notices that what Descartes has to say is remarkably similar to what Augustine had said (AT VII 197–8, 205; CSM II 139, 144). Descartes responds by casting the connection made by his readers as their finding authoritative support for his views (AT VII 219; CSM II 154). For another example, see letter to Mesland, May 2, 1644 (AT IV 113; CSMK III 232) Again, the implication is that Descartes has not borrowed from Augustine, but agrees that his view is supported by Augustine's. From the surviving texts, it is difficult to determine how much Descartes read of Augustine. In letters he eludes to two works (even quoting from one): *City of God* (letter to Mersenne, May 25, 1637, AT I 376 and the Colvius letter already cited) and *Confessions* (letter to Mesland, already cited). Secondary Sources: Menn (1995) and Mendelson (2012).

B

Beeckman, Isaac (1588–1637). Dutch physician and teacher. Descartes met Beeckman while serving in the military, in 1618. Descartes had joined the Army of Prince Maurice of Nassau, and was stationed in Breda, where Beeckman was then living. Scholars believe that Beeckman had a great influence on the young Descartes (he would have been 22 years old), rekindling in him an interest in science and mathematics. As a result of their friendship, Descartes wrote his first real work, *Compendium Musicae*.

Being (L. *esse*, *entis*). This concept has a long history in philosophy. As rooted in the Schools, a thing's *being* is the *what* of the thing. Generally, the *what* of a thing is the (essential) being of a thing that accounts for the thing's being the kind of thing it is. Thus, if *s* is *F*, and essentially so, then the being of *s* is *s*'s being *F*. According to Descartes, the *what* of a body, for example, is its extension in length, breadth, and depth. The *what* of a mind is its thinking or thought. Descartes sometimes uses the terms *being* (*entis* and sometimes *esse*) and *reality* (*realitas*) interchangeably. He also sometimes speaks of *a* being—for example, a body—where *being* (*entis*) or entity (*entia*) in such cases denotes a *thing* (*res*). In the *Principles*, he refers to extension as the nature and essence of body, and to thought as the nature and essence of mind (AT VIIIA 25; CSM I 210–1).

For Descartes, in line with Parmenides, the concept of being taken generally is importantly related to the concept of truth. In the Fifth Meditation, for example, Descartes writes: "whatever is true is something" (AT VII 65; CSM II 45). In comments about the Third Meditation, Descartes says, "Truth consists in *being*, and falsehood only in *non-being* . . ." (April 23, 1649 letter to Clerselier, AT V 356; CSMK III 377). Descartes recognizes two distinct kinds of being, formal and objective being (see the entry **Formal/Objective Reality**).

Body. See **Extension**.

Burman, Frans (1628–79). Dutch scholar. When around 20 years old, in 1648, he visited Descartes in the Netherlands and interviewed him. The interview can be found in AT V. Some of the interview has been translated into English, and can be found, for instance, in CSMK III, 332–54.

C

Caterus, Johannes (1590–1657). Dutch theologian. Caterus was a Catholic theologian who lived in Holland. He is author of the First Set of Objections of the *Meditations*.

Cause (L. *causa*; F. *cause*). The concept of causation has a long history in philosophy. No doubt when Descartes was in school he would have been taught the then-standard Aristotelian view of the four causes. They are a thing's *material*, *formal*, *efficient*, and *final* cause. Consider a house. The material cause of the house, Aristotle would say, is the material out of which the house is built. So, the bricks and wood, assuming the house was made out of these, constitute the material cause of the house. The formal cause of the house is the form or structure (its design) that the builder consulted in building the house. This structure guided the builder when placing the wooden beams, bricks, and so on. The efficient cause of the house is that which is responsible for its now being an existent house. This, of course, is the builder. Without the builder, there would be no house. Lastly, the final cause of the house is that for the sake of which the house is built. In other words, the final cause tells us what the purpose of a house is. A house is built for shelter. This is its final cause. Descartes breaks from this Aristotelian view. Instead, his natural philosophy recognizes, and deals exclusively in, *efficient* causes (see, e.g., AT VIIIA 15–6; CSM I 202–3).

Contemporaries of Descartes challenged him to be clearer about his views on causation. Princess Elisabeth, for example, pressed Descartes on how he conceived the possibility of the causal relationship between the mind and body. Several philosophers following in Descartes's wake also addressed the issue. Nicholas Malebranche, for example, showed concern over Descartes's notion of causation. Relatively recently scholars have done much to make Descartes's views clearer on this front. What is clear is that Descartes's view of efficient causation was a variation of what was called *transeunt* causation. This is sometimes cast as "event" causation, where one event is said to be the cause of another. One version of this view of causation has it that properties or qualities pass from cause to effect. This is sometimes called *influx* causation (also see **Formal/Eminent**). Descartes sometimes does talk as though he held some version of influx causation. For example, in the *Principles* he speaks of the transfer of motion (AT VIIIA 55; CSM I 234). But many scholars reject this reading of such texts. A fruitful interpretation that has emerged is one that casts Descartes's causal view as an "occasional" causal view (see, e.g., Nadler 1994). This is different from another doctrine with a similar name, *occasionalism*. Occasionalism, or one extreme version of it, tells us that finite beings (whether minds or bodies) have *no* causal powers. By contrast, occasional causation allows the possibility that finite bodies have such powers. The notion of an occasional cause is that, where A is said to be the cause of B, the presence (or existence) of A is sufficient for (immediately securing) the presence (or existence) of B. Secondary Sources: Nadler (1994), Schmaltz (2007), and Slowik (2013).

Certain, Certainty (L. *certi*, *certitudinem*; F. *certain*, *certainement*). These terms as used by Descartes have been a source of much contention among scholars. Descartes himself seems to recognize the troubles associated with them and the family of concepts they connote. This is suggested at the opening of the Second Meditation, where he makes a kind of joke about certainty: "I will proceed in this way until I recognize something certain, or, if nothing else, until I at least recognize for certain that there is no certainty" (AT VII 24; CSM II 16). Contentions aside, scholars agree that Descartes recognizes at least two kinds of certainty: metaphysical or absolute certainty, and moral certainty (AT VI 38, AT VII 144–5, AT VIIIA 327–8; CSM I 130, CSM II 103; CSM I 289–90).

In both kinds, certainty is an important indicator to one's having *knowledge*. "Knowledge," Descartes writes, "is certain cognition" (AT X 362; CSM I 10). It is not clear whether Descartes wishes to ultimately "locate" certainty in the cognitive *act* or in the *object* cognized (AT X 362–4; CSM I 10–3). In a reply to the Jesuit Pierre

Bourdin (1595–1653), Descartes says that although Bourdin took certainty as being in things, the things cognized, this would not be how he (Descartes) took it in the *Meditations*. He suggests that Bourdin should have instead treated doubt and certainty as "relations of our thought to objects" (AT VII 473; CSM II 318–9). This tilts the interpretative scale in favor of the view that certainty for Descartes was not in the objects cognized but in the acts of cognition. Even so, Descartes will speak of *propositions* as being certain (AT VI 33; CSM I 127), which are, in terms of cognition, a kind of object. He also will sometimes cast certainty as arising from a method or a science (*scientia*), arithmetic and geometry serving as the salient examples (AT X 366; CSM I 13). On this view, which is found in his early writings (e.g., in the *Rules*), certainty is importantly related to a *system* of interrelated propositions, arising from one's "seeing" or in one's becoming cognizant of the necessary connections that hold between the propositions that form the system. However, his most mature view casts certainty in terms of clear and distinct perception, where one is certain whenever one perceives something clearly and distinctly (AT VII 35, AT VIIIA 21–2; CSM II 24, CSM I 207–8).

He offers two formulations of the first kind of certainty, metaphysical or absolute certainty, which, for lack of better names, might be called a *negative* sense and a *positive* sense. In the negative sense, one is certain of *p*, or certain that *p* is true, whenever one believes or is convinced that not-*p* is impossible. "Absolute certainty," he writes, "arises when we believe that it is wholly impossible that something should be otherwise than we judge it to be" (AT VIIIA 328; CSM I 290). In the Third Meditation, Descartes considers what constitutes his being certain that "I am a thinking thing" is true, and writes, "In this first item of knowledge there is simply a clear and distinct perception of what I am asserting; this would not be enough to make me certain of the truth of the matter if it could ever turn out that something which I perceived with such clarity and distinctness was false" (AT VII 35; CSM II 24). This remark has been a source of contention among scholars, since the "first item" of knowledge that he mentions is not the existential claim of the *cogito*: "*I am, I exist*, is necessarily true whenever it is put forward by me or conceived in my mind" (AT VII 25; CSM II 17), but is "I am a thinking thing," which in the course of the *Meditations* comes after he had established the existential claim "I exist." A charitable reading, however, may take his point as follows. Descartes can be understood as telling the reader of the *Meditations* that the existential claim is (conceptually or logically) presupposed in the claim "I am thinking." Although presupposed, the claim "I exist" is not *deduced from* "I am thinking." In the Second Replies, for instance, he says that one "does not deduce existence from thought by means of a syllogism, but recognizes it as something self-evident by a simple intuition of the mind" (AT VII 140; CSM II 100). This intuition is one's insight of the fact "that it is impossible that he should think without existing" (*Ibid.*). This looks to tie directly into the negative sense of "absolute certainty," and suggests that certainty arises in one's seeing the "necessary connection" between "I am thinking" and "I exist," where the connection is shown to be necessary insofar as it is impossible to conceive the former while denying the latter. In terms of today's logic, such a relation between these two propositions would be cast as an entailment relation, and so his denying that the relation between these propositions is deductive in nature may be puzzling to today's reader. But Descartes dispels some of this, even in writings that predate the *Meditations*, where the insight into this sort of logical relation wrongly suggests a "movement" of the mind, where such movements occurs only in acts of deduction (AT X 370; CSM I 15). Instead, the relationship is understood in a single intuition of the mind—one perceives the connection all at once and not bit by bit (AT X 407; CSM I 37).

Descartes also sometimes speaks of certainty in the positive sense, where one is certain whenever one's will is compelled to assent to the truth of what one is thinking about. One is certain of *p*, or that *p* is true, whenever one's will is compelled to assent to *p*. Here, one's clearly and distinctly perceiving *p* is what prompts the compulsion (AT VII 36, 58–9; CSM II 25, 41). Some have argued that one's perceiving *p* clearly and distinctly is *coextensive with* the compelling of the will; they are one and the same cognitive event being described in two different ways. Be that as it may, the compelling of the will is spontaneous (*sponte*) or automatic. Descartes sometimes casts this compulsion in terms of *conviction*, when he is *convinced* or *persuaded* to believe something. "[A]s soon as we think that we correctly perceive something," he says, "we are spontaneously convinced (*persuademus*) that it is true" (AT VII 144; CSM II 103). Also, Descartes will even conjoin the positive and negative senses. He writes: "Now if this conviction is so firm that it is impossible for us ever to have any reason for doubting what we are convinced of, then there are no further questions for us to ask: we have everything that we could reasonably want . . . For the supposition which we are making here is of a conviction so firm that it is quite incapable of being destroyed; and such a conviction is clearly the same as the most perfect certainty" (AT VII 144; CSM II 103).

In the Third Meditation, Descartes notes that metaphysical or absolute certainty arises, for instance, when "considering something very simple and straightforward [as occurs] in arithmetic or geometry" (AT VII 35–6; CSM II 25). But, he reminds himself that by the close of the First Meditation he *was* able to doubt the propositions of arithmetic and geometry. But "the only reason for my later judgment that they were open to doubt," he says, "was that it occurred to me that perhaps some God could have given me a nature such that I was deceived even in matters which seemed most evident" (AT VII 36; CSM II 25). So, he was not able to *directly* conceive, for example, that *two added to three is not five*, for to conceive this is impossible—which is why it initially counted as something that was certain. But he was able to conceive that the *cause* of our intellectual faculty—a malevolent God, for instance—could have brought it about that this faculty simply could not conceive that *two added to three is not five*, even though such a possibility existed. So, even though he could not directly conceive the possibility of the contrary of *two added to three is five*, he could *indirectly* conceive it. But, as he goes on to argue in the Third Meditation, God exists, God cannot be a deceiver, and God is the author (origin) of our faculty of clear and distinct perception. Descartes summarizes the line of reasoning in the Second Replies: "Hence you see that once we have become aware that God exists it is necessary for us to imagine that he is a deceiver if we wish to cast doubt on what we clearly and distinctly perceive. And since it is impossible to imagine that he is a deceiver, whatever we clearly and distinctly perceive must be completely accepted as true and certain" (AT VII 144; CSM II 103).

In the second kind of certainty, moral certainty, although one is not absolutely certain, one may nevertheless possess some knowledge. In not being absolutely certain, however, it is possible to conceive alternatives that are opposed to what one is currently thinking. So, given that someone knows that one of two apples sitting on the table has been poisoned, but does not know which of the two apples is the poisoned apple, he or she may be inclined to not eat either. This inclination might arise from his or her having a desire to live (or to not die). But suppose that this person is stuck in that room and that the apples are all there are to eat. If this person does not eat, he or she will starve. Now what? Descartes says that this person's reasoning, decision, and eventual action must now deal in conjecture and probability. It is likely that the apple that this person chooses is not poisoned, but equally likely, at least from his or her epistemic point of view, that the apple chosen is the poisoned one. Both possibilities are equally probable in this case. The point is that this person must choose, but his or her decision and subsequent action are based on a certainty that is less reliable than absolute certainty—this lesser kind of certainty is what Descartes refers to as *moral certainty*. One is morally certain, Descartes says, in cases where one is not absolutely certain, but nevertheless knows something sufficiently to act in "ordinary life" (AT VIIIA 327; CSM I 289–90). In fact it is a kind of certainty that is sufficient for the *regulating* of one's behavior (AT VI 38; CSM I 130).

It is worth noting that the distinction that Descartes draws between metaphysical (or absolute) certainty and moral certainty is echoed by Gottfried Leibniz (1646–1716) in the *Monadology* (Articles 31–3), where he draws a distinction between *the principle of contradiction* and *the principle of sufficient reason*, which is in turn related to the distinction between the *truths of reasoning* and the *truths of fact*. But here it is important to note that Leibniz's principle of sufficient reason is deductive and not inductive. Even so, the contraries of the truths of fact are conceivable, unlike the truths of reasoning, which aligns with Descartes's moral and metaphysical certainty, respectively. The inductive mode of reasoning will appear again in David Hume's (1711–76) *Enquiry Concerning Human Understanding* (Section IV, Part I), where he draws a distinction between *relations of ideas* and *matters of fact*, and the kinds of reasoning each involves. Secondary Sources: Popkin (1960), Curley

(1978), Williams (1978), Wilson (1978), Lennon (2008), and Smith (2010b).

Circle, Cartesian. This is a problem originally proposed by Antoine Arnauld. In the *Meditations*, Descartes had established the "truth-rule" in connection to his clearly and distinctly perceiving something. "Whatever I perceive very clearly and distinctly is true" (AT VII 35; CSM II 24). He went on to use this rule to prove that God exists and is no deceiver. The trouble, however, as Arnauld saw it, was that the guarantee of the truth-rule was possible only *after* it was established that God exists and is no deceiver. But, the latter cannot be established without the guarantee of the truth-rule (AT VII 214; CSM II 150). Secondary Source: Lennon (2008).

Clarity and Distinctness/Obscurity and Confusion. *Clarity and distinctness* and *obscurity and confusion* are features that Descartes attributes to ideas or what he sometime calls *perceptions*. Taken individually, Descartes contrasts *clarity* with *obscurity* and *distinctness* with *confusion*. In what follows, we shall consider these concepts in light of three prevailing interpretations, followed by what we might call a *general* theory. But before doing this, let's briefly address a problem about which scholars have worried, namely, whether there is a difference between saying that one's perception of x is clear and distinct (an adjectival expression of these features) versus our saying that we clearly and distinctly perceive x (an adverbial expression of these features).

In his discussions of clear perceptions, especially in his later works, Descartes employs the adverb *clare*, as in one's "clearly perceiving x" (AT VII 43), though at other times he employs the adjective *clarus*, as in one's "having a clear perception of x" (AT VII 44). In addition to attributing clarity to the *act* of perception (adverbial) and to the perception itself (adjectival), he sometimes will speak of the *object* of the perception as being clear. In the *Principles*, Descartes says: "I call a perception 'clear' (*claram*) when it is present and accessible to the attentive mind—just as we say that we see something clearly (*clarè*) when it is present to the eye's gaze and stimulates it with a sufficient degree of strength and accessibility" (AT VIIIA 22; CSM I 207). Some scholars have emphasized the adjectival form of *clear* (or the substantival *clarity*), while others have emphasized the adverbial form (*clearly*). Some have argued that the interpretive conflict between the adverbial and adjectival reading of *clarity* shows that there really is no theory here. That is, their claim is that Descartes did not work under any theory of clear (and distinct) perception.

Be that as it may, these senses need not be opposed, and there is a way to tie the two together. Suppose that one goes to the eye doctor. Also suppose that in order to examine one's visual acuity the doctor asks the patient to look at a black dot painted on the white office wall (the wall is located in front of the patient). As the doctor tries various lenses (inserting them in front of the patient's eyes), the patient is asked to tell the doctor when the black dot is maximally clear, where by being maximally clear it is meant that the contrast of the edge of the black dot and the white wall are sharpest. Noting something about the *object* of vision informs the doctor about the *act* of vision. The more clear the object (adjectival) seen, the more clearly one sees (adverbial). It will be helpful, in understanding Descartes, to keep this sort of thing in mind. In what follows, then, no important philosophical difference will be drawn between the above two phrasings.

There are several versions of the theory of clarity and distinctness in the secondary literature. With the exception of one of the theories to be considered shortly, these theories only imply or only suggest the concepts of obscurity and confusion. As we shall see, one of the theories is best understood by beginning with the concepts of obscurity and confusion and constructing clarity and distinctness from them. Let's now move to considering the three prevailing interpretations mentioned earlier.

Compulsion Theory. The first interpretation (most clearly articulated by Curley) is what has been called the *compulsion theory*. This theory is grounded in what Descartes says in the Fourth and Fifth Meditations (AT VII 59, 62, 65; CSM II 41, 43, 45). Here, the theory tells us that one clearly perceives that s is F whenever one's will is compelled to affirm it. In other words, we find that we *must* ascribe F to s. If one's will is not compelled to ascribe F

to s, one's perception (by default) is obscure—one perceives s's being F obscurely. It will be important to keep in mind that there is a difference between one's *not being compelled* to ascribe F to s and one's *being compelled not to ascribe* F to s. With respect to the former, one *could* ascribe F to s, even though one is not compelled to do so. With respect to the latter, however, the possibility of ascribing F to s is off the table, so to speak. To be compelled not to ascribe F to s is akin to *denying* that F belongs to s. With this difference in mind, where $G \neq F$, one distinctly perceives that s is F whenever one is compelled to ascribe F to s (and so the perception is clear) *and* is compelled not to ascribe G to s. Notice this second criterion, the one that states that one is compelled not to ascribe G to s (keeping in mind that this is different from not being compelled to ascribe), is crucial for a perception's being distinct. Also notice that all distinct perceptions will meet the condition for being clear, but not vice versa. So, all distinct perceptions are clear. But, it will not be the case that all clear perceptions must be distinct. Thus, the compulsion theory tells us that we clearly and distinctly perceive that s is F (or, our perception that s is F is clear and distinct) whenever we are compelled to ascribe F to s, but at the same time we are compelled not to ascribe other things to s, such as G, where $F \neq G$. In such cases, F would be considered s's nature or essence.

So, consider what Descartes says in the Synopsis of the *Meditations*. The natures of mind and body "are not only different, but in some way opposite" (AT VII 13; CSM II 10). He banks on this in the Sixth Meditation when arguing for the real distinction between mind and body (AT VII 78; CSM II 54) (for more on this, see **Distinction, Real**). Consider, then, the (innate) idea of body. According to the compulsion theory, we clearly and distinctly perceive that body is extended (or, our perception that body is extended is clear and distinct) since we are compelled to ascribe extension to body (i.e., we *must* ascribe extension to body), but at the same time we are compelled not to ascribe thought or thinking to body. Likewise with our (innate) idea of mind. We clearly and distinctly perceive that mind is thinking (or, our perception that mind is thinking is clear and distinct) since we are compelled to ascribe thinking or thought to mind (i.e., we must ascribe thinking to mind), but at the same time we are compelled not to ascribe extension to mind.

Compatibility Theory. A second theory (most clearly articulated by Alanen) is what has been called the *compatibility theory.* This theory deemphasizes compulsion of the will, and so ignores what is said in the Fourth Meditation (and so parts ways with the compulsion theory), though it finds support in the Fifth Meditation, and finds further support in Descartes's responses to critics (AT VII 116, 152; CSM II 83, 108). Here, the theory tells us that one clearly and distinctly perceives that *s* is *F* (or, one's perception that *s* is *F* is clear and distinct), whenever one perceives that *s*'s being *F* is not incompatible with existence. In other words, one perceives that *s* (its being *F*) is a possible object. Notice that unlike the compulsion theory, there are not separate criteria here for clarity and distinctness. The existential compatibility condition is a sign of both features (clarity and distinctness). If, in perceiving *s*'s being *F*, one perceives that *s*'s nature is not compatible with existence (i.e., one perceives that *s* is an impossible object), then one's idea of *s*'s being *F* is obscure and confused—one perceives *s* obscurely and confusedly. Return to our example of the (innate) idea of body. One clearly and distinctly perceives that body is extended since, when thinking about the nature of body, one perceives that such a thing (an extended thing) is not incompatible with existence (i.e., one perceives that body is a possible object).

Attention-Grabber Theory. A third theory (most clearly articulated by Nelson) finds support in the *Principles.* Recall that Descartes says, "I call a perception 'clear' when it is present and accessible to the attentive mind . . ." (AT VIIIA 21–2; CSM I 207–8). This theory's view of clarity is, perhaps ironically, better understood by starting with the concept of obscurity. One obscurely perceives that *s* is *F* (or, one's perception that *s* is *F* is obscure) whenever there is some other feature, *G*, not identical to *F*, that hinders one's mental view of the relation between *s* and *F*. Not only can ideational features get in the way, but also so can mental activity. Both can serve to divert one's attention away from our "seeing" that *s* is *F*. The less obscure a perception—that is, the less that *G* obscures from mental view *s*'s relation to *F*—the clearer it is. The clearer a perception, the more it "grabs" one's attention. Thus, one clearly perceives *s* is *F* whenever *s*'s being *F* grabs one's attention. Here, clarity is scalar, and is always understood in terms of more or less. The more strongly the content of the idea "grabs" one's attention, the more clearly one perceives the ideational content. But, as just noted, if there are any ideational elements or moments of mental activity that serve to divert one's attention away from the idea in question (here, the idea of s's being F), the contents are less clear or less clearly perceived. As noted, to perceive s less (and less) clearly is another way of saying that one perceives s more (and more) obscurely. Related to this, one confusedly perceives s (or, one's perception of s is confused) whenever other ideational elements (which may or may not obscure s) are present in the idea of s. The attention-grabber theory takes the Latin *confusio* literally, and the ideational elements are *mix together* in the idea of s. The more isolated s is (in thought) from other ideational elements, the more distinct the idea or perception of s becomes. Thus, one perceives s distinctly whenever one perceives s in isolation from other ideational elements. This aligns with what Descartes says in the *Principles*: "I call a perception 'distinct' if, as well as being clear, it is so sharply separated from all other perceptions that it contains only what is clear" (AT VIIIA 22; CSM I 207–8). One implication of this theory is that no (or certainly very few) ideas are *perfectly* clear and distinct.

General Theory. Descartes refers to the elements of our ideas, the items that constitute the contents of ideas, as *simple natures*. *Extension* is a simple nature, as is *shape* and *size*. So is *color* and *sound* (for more, see **Simple Nature**). There is a general theory of clarity and distinctness that aligns with (and in fact relates) the three prevailing interpretations introduced earlier. Let's start by briefly considering the method that Descartes uses to analyze his ideas.

Descartes analyzes his ideas (their contents) by an interesting method of classifying, or *enumerating* as he calls it (for more, see **Enumeration**). The analysis is done by comparing ideational elements, the simple natures, for similarity (AT X 439–40; CSM I 57–8). Simple natures are similar when they share a *common nature* (for more, see **Common Nature**). When two simple natures share a common nature (i.e., they are similar or are identical in some respect), they are classified in the same category (or class). According to Descartes, an analysis of the contents of our ideas will yield a very basic category scheme, consisting of two mutually exclusive classes of object: the class of *thinking things* and the class of *extended things*.

Understood this way, the enumeration looks to prefigure what today is called a *logical partition*. The gist of this is that all modes (qualities or properties) will fall into either the class of thinking things, or the class of extended things, but never both. Here is how clarity and distinctness are related to Descartes's theory of enumeration. This has been called the *general theory*.

In his interview with Frans Burman (1628–79), Descartes says that although we can clearly imagine a chimera that had the head of a lion and the body of a goat, we do not (and cannot) clearly *perceive* such a thing, since we do not perceive the "link" that binds or unites these things together (AT V 160; CSMK III 343–4). The suggestion is that in order to perceive something clearly, we must perceive the relation that unites the elements of the idea (the simple natures) into a single, unified essence or nature. Here, "uniting" simply means that the simple natures share a common nature. By contrast, then, one perceives something obscurely whenever one fails to perceive any such relation. As Descartes argues in the *Principles*, for example, sensory ideas (such as the sensory idea of the Sun) will never be clear (i.e., they will always be obscure), since there is no intelligible relation that *can* be perceived that holds between color, say, and motion. We might infer a correlation between them (color and motion), but we will not perceive any relation that unites them into a single nature (AT VIIIA 322; CSM I 285). That is, we see that they do not share a common nature. Thus if our sensory idea of the Sun, for instance, contains the simple natures yellow and circular-shaped (and it does), and there is no relation that we can perceive that holds between them such that they are united into a single nature, then the sensory idea of the Sun is not clear. It will be obscure.

Burman presses Descartes further on the notion of clarity. Descartes's answer further confirms the view that for an idea to be clear we must perceive the "link" (the relation or common nature) that unites the simple natures contained in the idea into a single nature. Suppose, Burman says, that an idea is composed of two simpler ideas, where these simpler ideas are clear. Is clarity transitive, so that if these simpler ideas are clear, the composite idea is also clear? Burman sees that if Descartes answers this in the affirmative, there are real troubles lurking. He supposes the case where our idea of a finite being is clear, as is our idea of an infinite being, where the two have been conjoined to form a new idea—the idea of a finite–infinite being. If clarity is transitive, then the idea of a finite–infinite being would also be clear! This would be a bad consequence of Descartes's theory of clarity, since a finite–infinite being is an impossible being, like a square–circle. Descartes agrees. He replies, "Even if those ideas are clear when taken apart, they are certainly not clear when joined together. Your idea is thus very obscure, for the conception you have of the combination and unity of the two ideas is not clear but extremely obscure" (AT V 160; CSMK III 343–4). So, reconsider the sensory idea of the Sun. The suggestion is that even if the ideas of circular-shaped and yellow were clear taken separately, the composite idea of a circular-shaped yellow thing (the Sun) would not be clear, for there is no relation that can be perceived that would unite these items into a single being. The general theory, then, tells us that the idea of s is clear whenever one recognizes the simple natures that constitute the idea of s, and recognizes the relation that "binds" them together, making them a singular, unified essence.

An idea is *distinct* whenever it contains only those simple natures falling under one but not both of the mutually exclusive divisions (categories or classes) of the enumeration. The two mutually exclusive divisions, recall, are *thinking* and *extension*. Thus, if an idea of a body contained only the simple natures size, shape, motion, which are natures falling under the category (class) *extension*, this idea is distinct. To use the earlier example, our (innate) idea of body is clear because we perceive that relation (common nature) that unites the simple natures present in the idea into a single essence. Size, shape, and motion, simple natures included in this idea, modify one and the same attribute: extension. One way to express this is that each satisfies "x modifies the same attribute of y," which is a "relational" way of expressing the common nature. The (innate) idea of body is also distinct, since it includes only those simple natures that fall under (or are members of) the class of extended things. By contrast, the sensory idea of the Sun is obscure and confused, since there is no relation (common nature) perceived that unifies the simple natures included in the idea into a single essence, and the idea includes simple natures, for example *yellow* and *circular-shaped*, that fall under (or are members of) the classes of thinking and of extended things. The simple natures in this sense are (*confusio*) "mix together."

Generally, Descartes's theory of clear and distinct perception suggests that ideas can be (1) clear and distinct, (2) clear and confused, (3) obscure and confused, but never (4) obscure and distinct. This last possibility is banned, so to speak, since distinctness is understood in terms of (or is parasitic on) clarity. But a problem lurks. What about clear and confused ideas? How is such an idea even possible? Descartes actually gives an example of a clear and confused idea: the sensory idea of pain in some body part (AT VIIIA 22; CSM I 208). This is an idea that includes the simple nature pain and various simple natures such as shape, size, location, and so on. Why isn't this idea obscure? For, as in the case of our sensory idea of the Sun, which was said to be obscure precisely because we do not perceive a relation (common nature) that serves to unify them into a single essence, why isn't the sensory idea of pain in a body part obscure for the same reason?

Recall Descartes's remark to Burman about our clearly imagining a chimera. There, he says that although we can clearly imagine the chimera (which in this case is imagined to have the head of a lion and body of a goat), we cannot clearly perceive the chimera since we do not perceive the link (common nature) that unifies these parts into a single essence. Here, the distinction is between clearly imagining (or clear imagination) and clearly perceiving (or clear perception), where the latter refers to pure intellection. Imagination, as Descartes says elsewhere, in addition to mind requires a body (or extension) (see, e.g., AT VII 72–3; CSM II 50–1). Pure intellection does not require a body. The clarity associated with imagination might be called a weak sense of "clarity," and might be tentatively defined as follows: The idea or perception of s is *clear* in the weak sense whenever the idea includes simple natures that (hypothetically) form the nature of s. (We'll use "hypothetical" since it may turn out that there is no such nature. Think of *hypothetical* in this context as expressing "possible." So, a hypothetical nature is a possible nature.) The hypothetical nature of the chimera, then, is that it has the head of a lion and body of a goat. Of course, a new problem now arises. For, if all ideas exhibit hypothetical natures, then all ideas will be clear in the weak sense. But what about Burman's example of the idea of a finite–infinite being? Don't we want to say that this is not clear, not even in the weak sense? There is a remedy. Descartes says that ideas that are put together with contradictory ideas do not express natures—period—not even what we are calling hypothetical ones (AT VII 71, 152; CSM II 50, 108). Thus, if all ideas are clear in the weak sense whenever they exhibit hypothetical natures, and the ideas of impossible objects (i.e., ideas put together with contradictory ideas) do not exhibit hypothetical natures, then it follows that such ideas are not clear even in the weak sense. So, we now have a sense in which ideas will be obscure, and will not be clear (not even in the weak sense).

When Descartes introduces the sensory idea of pain in a body part as his example of a clear and confused idea, then, instead of taking "clear" in the strong sense, which would require us to perceive a relation (common nature) that unifies the pain and body part into a single essence, we can take "clear" in the weak sense. The idea of pain in a body part is clear in the same sense as the idea of that chimera. Every idea that is clear in the strong sense will be clear in the weak sense, but not vice versa. There is a sense, then, in which an idea that is clear in the strong sense is *clearer* than an idea that is clear only in the weak sense. As the attention-grabber theory makes clear, Descartes speaks of clarity in scalar terms (in terms of more and less), and the strong and weak senses of "clarity" just introduced preserve that way of talking. Secondary Sources: Wilson (1978), Curley (1986), Bolton (1986), Alanen (1994), Nelson (1997), and Smith (2001, 2010b).

Cogito ergo sum. This is the Latin version of Descartes's now-famous phrase, "I am thinking, therefore I am." It is found stated in the *Discourse on the Method* (AT VI 32–3; CSM I 127). However, the *Discourse* was first published in French. So, the phrase first appeared in print as *"Je pense, donc je suis."* It is not actually found in the *Meditations*, though in the Second Meditation Descartes works out the philosophical import of the insight it expresses (AT VII 25; CSM II 16–7). In the Second Set of Replies, Descartes tells his critics, who had reminded him of what he had written in the *Discourse*, that one does not derive one's existence from any sort of syllogism, "but recognizes it as something self-evident by a simple intuition of the mind" (AT VII 140; CSM II 100). As some scholars have noted, the Second Meditation version of the *cogito*, as it is called, is better understood as a performance. By performing this exercise as laid out in the First and Second Meditations, the meditator is led to the insight that he or she exists so long as he or she thinks. Other critics noted that this very insight could be found in Augustine (see, e.g., AT VII 97–8; CSM II 139. Also see letter to Mersenne, December 1640, AT III 261; CSMK III 161). In his response, Descartes seems to downplay any suggestion that he borrowed from Augustine, and recasts the connection as his critics offering support of his view by point out that authoritative figures such as Augustine had said similar things. Secondary Source: Hintikka (1962).

Common Nature (L. *natura communis*). A common nature is that which objects have in common (AT X 439–40, 449–50; CSM I 57, 63). Objects that share a common nature are *similar*. Common natures are like equivalence relations, which when applied to objects of inquiry will sort those objects into an enumeration (which is like a logical partition). Equivalence relations have three important properties: they are reflexive, symmetric, and transitive (for more, see **Common Notion** and **Enumeration**). All bodies, for example, share a common nature: they are extended in length, breadth, and depth.

Common Notion (L. *communes notiones*). Early in his career, Descartes casts common notions as relational properties (i.e., as properties of relations), and sometimes as relations themselves: "[T]hey are [as it were] links which connect other simple natures together" (AT X 419; CSM I 45; for more, see **Simple Nature**). Understood as relational properties, they can account for the ability of a common nature to sort objects into an enumeration. An enumeration is akin to a logical partition (see **Enumeration**). Descartes provides examples of two common notions (as relational properties): "'things that are the same as a third thing are the same as each other': 'things that cannot be related in the same way to a third thing are different in some respect.'" (AT X 419; CSM I 45) Although not perfect formulations, these are akin to the sorts of relational properties attributed to equivalence relations that account for their being able to sort objects into logical partitions, namely, the properties of reflexivity, symmetry, and transitivity.

Later, in the Second Replies of the *Meditations*, Descartes casts common notions as axioms (of his system) (AT VII 164–6; CSM II 16–7). In the *Principles*, he casts common notions as "eternal truths" that "reside within our mind" (AT VIIIA 23; CSM I 209). Examples of such truths are: "*nothing comes from nothing; it is impossible for the same thing to be and not to be at the same time*; and, *what is done cannot be undone*" (AT VIIIA 24; CSM I 209). This way of casting common notions looks interestingly similar to what Hume, in his *Inquiry Concerning Human Understanding*, would later call *Relations of Ideas*. But whereas Hume would not hold these to be innate, Descartes will. Despite this important difference, the following are similarities worth noting: (1) the truth of such a common notion (or relations of idea proposition) is self-evident or can be determined by reason alone, (2) the opposite of a common notion is a contradiction (see, e.g., AT IV 444; CSMK III 290), and (3) its truth can be known independently of sensory experience.

Conscience/Conscious. This term looks originally to have arisen in moral discourse. When speaking of one's awareness of one's doing what is best, Descartes uses *conscience* (French) (AT IV 266; CSMK III 258, August 4, 1645 letter to Elisabeth) In another letter (to Elisabeth) he speaks of Socrates's "inner voice," which looks to be related to the notion of conscience. Although here he doesn't use the term (contrary to how CSMK translates the passage). When speaking of being aware or acquainted with something, he uses *conscios* (Latin) (AT V 221, July 29, 1648 letter to Arnauld). In the Second Replies, when again speaking about being aware of something, he uses the Latin *conscii* and *conscius* (AT VII 160; CSM II 113).

Corporeal Substance. See **Extension**.

Creation (L. *creatione*; F. *creation*). The concept of creation has its origin in theology (or religion more generally). It is traditionally understood to be a *divine act* or *action*. Even so, conceptually speaking it is not like others acts. The "logic" of act–talk casts an act as having a beginning, a middle, and an end: conceptually speaking, an act (or action) is something that must be performed over some interval of time. Where "*S*" is the performer of an act, and "*A*" is a typical act or action, it is always possible to ask, "What happened *before* S performed A?," "What happened *after* S performed A?," and so on. *Production* is an example of a typical kind of act or action. Consider the case in which *S* is said to produce *P*, where the act of *S*'s producing *P* is *A*. So, we can rephrase *S*'s producing *P* as *S performs A*. The "logic" of act–talk allows us to ask, for example, what *S* was doing, or what was happening, prior to or before *S* produced *P* (or before *S* performed *A*). The concept of production requires that *P*, the thing produced, is produced out of items that existed in some form prior to *P*'s production. *P* is said to be produced out of or from those items. This aligns with the conceptual requirement for there to be a before (the beginning) and after (the ending) the act of *P*'s being produced. On this front, creation is in stark contrast to production (and other acts). Unlike the production of *P*, the creation of *P* does not require there to be any preexisting items out of which or from which *P* is created. In other words, *P* can be created *ex nihilo*—*from nothing or out of nothing!* Time was considered one of the items of the cosmos that God creates. Time cannot be *produced*. For, production of time would require there to exist items out of which or from which time was produced, items that existed prior to or before its production. But clearly there is a profound conceptual muddle in our asking, "What came before time?" We cannot conceive of there being a *before* time (assuming "before" is a temporal concept), so we cannot conceive of there being items existing prior to or before time, items out of which time was produced. No, time is created! Also, as with all things created, it was created *ex nihilo*. Augustine (in *Confessions*, Book XI) considers several interesting conceptual problems that arise in our trying to conceive of the creation of the universe, where time is one of the items in question. In this sense, creation *qua* divine act was considered a mystery or miracle.

Philosophically speaking, Descartes saw creation of something *ex nihilo* as being only conceptually or rationally distinct from God's preserving or conserving that same something over some period of time. "For a lifespan," he says in the Third Meditation, "can be divided into countless parts, each completely independent of the others, so that it does not follow from the fact that I existed a little while ago that I must exist now, unless there is some cause which as it were creates me afresh at this moment—that is, which preserves me. For it is quite clear to anyone who attentively considers the nature of time that the same power and action are needed to preserve anything at each individual moment of its duration as would be required to create that thing anew if it were not yet in existence" (AT VII 49; CSM II 33). In the Third Set of Replies, Descartes says that the idea of God's creating the world is conceptually derived from our understanding that all finite things ultimately depend on the infinite (AT VII 188; CSM II 132)—as he will say in other places, the finite presupposes the infinite, where the latter is said to make possible the former (e.g., AT VII 45; CSM II 31). Insofar as all things depend ultimately on God's concurrence, and the latter is only conceptually distinct from creation, then this is a sense in which we conceive of God's creating all things. But notice that this is not some image or picture of God's *doing* something. That is, we are not confusedly imagining God at his workbench, prior to creating the world, which will include creating time (time being the duration of things), where God presumably *does* something, where—poof!—from this act all things, including time, result. That would be to wrongly cast creation as a kind of production. Even so, in the Sixth Set of Replies, Descartes, in speaking about the creation of the world, casts it as something that God willed "in time" (AT VII 432; CSM II 291). This discussion is related to other items that God is said to have created, items that are cast as being *eternal*, which does more than to suggest that they are not temporal (for more, see **Eternal Truths**).

D

Distinction, Modal (L. *distinctio modalis*; F. *distinction modale*). A modal distinction is a distinction made between a mode and the substance that possesses the mode, or between two or more modes of the same substance (AT VIIIA 30; CSM I 214). The first version of this distinction is based upon the fact that "we can clearly perceive a substance apart from the mode which we say differs from it, whereas we cannot, conversely, understand the mode apart from the substance" (*Ibid.*). Consider a spherical-shaped body. The idea is that we can consider (i.e., conceive) something's being a body, which requires us to conceive it as being extended, minus its having this specific shape (so, minus its being spherical), but we cannot conceive a thing's being spherical minus its being extended (i.e., minus its being a body). This shows that there is an important sense in which the shape, in this case the mode, depends for its being on the being of the substance, in this case an extended thing, or a body, in a way that its being a body (its being extended) does not depend for its being on the being of this specific shape. The second version of this distinction focuses on a difference between two modes of the same substance. For example, we make a modal distinction when we draw a distinction between a body's shape and its motion (*Ibid.*). A modal distinction also holds between modes of two different substances. For example, *doubting*, which is a mode of mind, and *shape*, which is a mode of body, are modally distinct. This, Descartes argues, is importantly different from the modal distinction drawn between modes of two substances of the same kind—for instance, when we draw a distinction between the shape of one body and that of another. The difference is that in the former case we can also conceive the two substances, mind and body, completely independently of one another, in which case the distinction might be better cast as a real distinction (for more, see **Distinction, Real**). Secondary Sources: Wilson (1978), Curley (1986), Nelson (1996, 1997), and Smith (2001, 2010b).

Distinction, Rational or Conceptual (L. *distinctio rationis*; F. *distinction raison*). A rational distinction, sometimes translated as *conceptual distinction*, is "a distinction between a substance and some attribute of that substance without which the substance is unintelligible; alternatively, it is a distinction between two such attributes of a single substance" (AT VIIIA 30; CSM I 214). The idea is that the distinction one draws between an attribute and the substance that has this attribute, or between two attributes of the same substance, is purely conceptual or mental. "Such a distinction is recognized," Descartes says, "by our inability to form a clear and distinct idea of the substance if we exclude from it the attribute in question, or alternatively, by our inability to perceive clearly the idea of one of the two attributes if we separate it from the other" (*Ibid.*). For example, one could not clearly and distinctly conceive of extension, the principal attribute of body, and at the same time completely exclude from this idea the idea of the substance that has this attribute. Since extension is that attribute that accounts for the very intelligibility of a body, or a corporeal substance, were one to separate (the idea of) extension, or to exclude it as he says, from (the idea of) the substance, the ideas would be rendered unintelligible. For, in the case of the idea of extension excluded from the idea of substance, the former would be the idea of an extended nothing, which is a contradiction (see the entry for **Vacuum**). So, it would not be an idea of an anything. In the case of the idea of substance excluded from the idea of extension, the former would be, to paraphrase John Locke, an idea of a "something we know not what." Again, this would not be an idea of anything. As Descartes puts it, "we cannot initially become aware of a substance merely through its being an existing thing, since this alone does not itself have any effect on us" (AT VIIIA 25; CSM I 210). One becomes aware of a substance by way of becoming aware of one of its attributes (*Ibid.*). Now, "a substance may indeed be known through any attribute at all; but each substance has one principal property which constitutes its nature and essence, and to which all its other properties are referred" (*Ibid.*). In the case of body or corporeal substance, that attribute, its *principal attribute*, is extension (in length, breadth, and depth). It is what accounts for the intelligibility of body. So, although one can focus on (the idea of this body's) extension while ignoring (the idea of) substance (where the substance is understood as that on which the attribute ontologically depends), which would be a case of abstraction, one cannot exclude (the idea of) this substance from (the idea of) extension. As Descartes also notes, the same will hold for attributes of the same substance. For example, one can focus (in an idea) on a body's extension while ignoring its duration (its existence over time), but one cannot exclude (the idea of) this body's extension from (the idea of) this body's duration, "since a substance cannot cease to endure without also ceasing to be" (AT VIIIA 30; CSM I 214) (for more, see the entries for **Abstract/Abstraction/Exclusion**). What rational or conceptual distinction is supposed to show is that if two things are only rationally distinct, then not only is it that we cannot clearly and distinctly conceive them in complete isolation from one another (for, in trying to do so we render them unintelligible), but also they cannot *exist* separately or in isolation from one another. This shows that such items would not be *really distinct* (for more see **Distinction, Real**). Secondary Sources: Nolan (1997a, 1997b), Smith (2010a).

Distinction, Real (L. *distinctio realis*; F. *distinction réelle*). A real distinction holds "only between two or more substances; and we can perceive that two substances are really distinct simply from the fact that we can clearly and distinctly understand one apart from the other" (AT VIIIA 28; CSM I 213). It is not clear whether substances of the same kind are really distinct. So, for example, it is not clear whether two bodies are really distinct from one another. This is so because we cannot clearly and distinctly understand one apart from the other. To be able to clearly and distinctly understand them apart, we would have to be able to conceive one in complete isolation from the other. In other words, we would have to be able to *exclude* (in thought) one from the other (see the entry for **Exclusion**). But, this cannot be done, for the nature of both is extension. Thus, when we conceive the nature of the one body, we conceive the nature of the other. Even so, Descartes says that the parts of a body are really distinct from one another (*Ibid.*), which does more than to suggest that a real distinction can hold between two bodies, and so can hold between substances of the same kind. This is a controversial issue that has arisen among scholars. Some argue that there are corporeal substances (plural), where they are really distinct from one another. Others argue that there is only one corporeal substance, where "bodies" are at best only modally distinct from one another. Spinoza interpreted Descartes this way. This view emphasizes Descartes's saying that the parts of the body in question are only "separated" in thought, or as Descartes puts is, "delimited by us in our thought" (*Ibid.*). Of course, the same issue arises when considering mind. Are individual minds really distinct from one another? The question is further complicated by Descartes's view that finite (human) minds are individuated in part by way of their relationship to body (e.g., see the February 9, 1645 letter to Mesland, AT IV 166–7; CSMK III 242–3). Some of the disagreement among scholars is in part resolved by a consideration of Descartes's view of what he calls adequate and inadequate, or complete and incomplete, ideas of substance (for more, see the entry **Idea, Adequate/Inadequate**). However, all scholars would appear to agree that for Descartes *mind* and *body* are really distinct substances. For, we can clearly and distinctly conceive the nature of mind independently of our conceiving the nature of body, and vice versa. This distinction is crucial to Descartes's argument in the Sixth Meditation that concludes that mind and body can exist independently of one another (AT VII 78; CSM II 54). So, it plays an important role in Descartes's attempt at establishing his dualism. Secondary Sources: Nolan (1997a, 1997b), Hoffman (2002b), Smith (2010a).

E

Emotion (L. *affectus, commotiones*; F. *affection, commotion, émotion*). Descartes's earliest reference to what has been translated into English as *emotion* is found in *Cogitationes Privatæ* ("Private Thoughts," AT X 213–48). Some of these texts date back to 1619. The word that Descartes uses is the Latin *affectus* (AT X 217). Here, the view is that an affection manifests in a thing when a thing is *affected by*, or we might even say, *altered by*, something else. Descartes specifically offers one's *being angered* (*irascitur*) as an example of such an affection. He also refers to such an affection in this text as a *passion* (*passione*) (AT X 217), a term that he will use throughout his career. Generally, the result of one's being altered in some way by something else is a *passion*, where the view is that the something doing the altering is the agent and the one being affected is the patient. The agent is active; the patient is passive. Even so, it is not clear why CSM translates this as *emotion*. The more accurate translation would be the English *affection*, which is more interpretively (or theoretically) neutral than *emotion*.

In the Latin version of the *Meditations* (1641), when discussing the various kinds of thoughts that he has, Descartes again uses *affectus*, where in this context he lists *fear* (the Latin is *timeo*—"I fear") as an example of such a thought (AT VII 37; CSM II 26). In the

French version of the *Meditations*, which Descartes did not translate but approved, the Latin term is translated into French as *affections* (AT IX 29). Again, CSM translates this as *emotion*. There is a letter to Pollot, dated January 1641, in which Descartes actually uses the French *l'émotion* and the phrase *cette émotion* (*this emotion*) (AT III 280). In the letter, Descartes consoles Pollot about the death of Pollot's brother, where Descartes identifies the "internal disturbance that nature has aroused" in Pollot to be sadness (*la tristesse*) (AT X 280). Given that the French translation of the *Meditations* and the letter to Pollot emerge around the same time, one wonders why Descartes instead approves *affections* in the French translation of the *Meditations* and does not insist on *émotion*, the latter used in the letter to Pollot. One possible explanation is that the Latin *affectus* and the French *affection* keep the discussion located squarely within the domain of metaphysics, while the French *émotion* may have been taken to connote something more appropriately located in a psychological or even a moral discussion. We get some evidence for this in the *Principles*, for instance, when Descartes introduces the term *mode*, where ". . . we employ the term *mode* when we are thinking of a substance as being affected or modified . . ." (AT VIIIA 26). In this sense, shape and motion, modes of body, are as much affections as are the thoughts of fear and sadness, which are modes of (embodied) mind.

But also in the *Principles*, published originally in Latin (1644), Descartes uses the terms *commotiones*, *pathemata*, and *commotio* (e.g., AT VIIIA 23). The Latin *commotiones* is later translated in the French version as *commotion*, which means *violent motion* or *violent movement*, and the Latin *pathemata* (actually this term has Greek origins) is translated as *passions* (AT VIIIA 23). We in fact do not see the French *les émotions* and *l'émotion* officially introduced (i.e., introduced in work intended for publication) until the French translation of the *Principles* (AT IXB 45), but as was the case with the *Meditations* it is important to note that Descartes was not this text's translator. Claude Picot (1601–68) translated the text, the French translation of the *Principles* published in 1647, 3 years after the original Latin. Although Descartes approved the translation (AT IXB 1–20; CSM I 179–90), it is likely that it was Picot and not Descartes who introduced the term *l'émotion*.

In any event, the term *emotion* clearly connotes motion or movement, which may be why CSM uses it. In the *Passions of the Soul* (1649), Descartes develops a view of the passions. Although not perfectly clear, a passion is cast as a thought in the mind (or soul) that arises from specific motions in the brain (here, it is the motions of the fine particles constituting the animal spirits) (AT XI 349; CSM I 339). It is a passion insofar as the mind (or soul) is affected by the body, the body acting as agent. The passions serve a specific purpose, namely, "they dispose our soul to want the things which nature deems useful for us (as humans)" (AT XI 372; CSM I 349). In other places, Descartes says that the *effect* of the passions on the soul is that "they move and dispose the soul to want the things for which they prepare the body" (AT XI 359; CSM I 343). The view that the passions *move* a person to perform some action is no doubt related to their sometimes being later referred to as *emotions*. Love, for example, is a passion or emotion that compels us toward the object loved, while hate is a passion or emotion that compels us to move away from the object hated (AT XI 387; CSM I 356). Unlike our sensory ideas, passions presuppose in their makeup some reference to what is good or bad for the human being. They express what we might think of as a utilitarianesque value, what is good (and in many cases this will be accompanied by *pleasure*) is that which promotes the preservation of the union of mind and body (the human being), what is bad (in many cases this will be accompanied by *pain*) is that which threatens the preservation of the union. Secondary Sources: Blom (1979) and Rutherford (2013).

Ends/Purpose/Teleology. The notion of an end or goal-directed action was part of Aristotle's theory of causation. There were four distinct kinds of cause: (1) formal, (2) material, (3) efficient, and (4) final. The notion of an end or goal-directed action fell under (4), *final cause* (for more on this, see the entry **Cause**). Descartes explicitly rejects our ever being able to come to know the final causes, or purposes, of natural things, let alone the final cause or purpose of the entire cosmos. In the Fourth Meditation, he says that in light of God's immense, incomprehensible, and infinite intellect, "I consider the customary search for final causes to be totally useless in physics . . ." (AT VII 55; CSM II 39). In the Fifth Replies, Descartes suggests that Gassendi, author of the Fifth Set of Objections, seemed to have confused arguments in defense of the notion of a final cause for those that would be better taken as defending the notion of an efficient cause. That said, Descartes allows some room for final causation. "In ethics," he says, ". . . where we may often legitimately employ conjectures, it may admittedly be pious on occasion to try to guess what purpose God may have had in mind in his direction of the universe; but in physics, where everything must be backed up by the strongest arguments, such conjectures are futile" (AT VII 375; CSM II 258).

Enumeration (L. *enumeratione*). Descartes introduces this concept in one of his earliest works, the *Rules*. It plays an important role in his method, and can be found employed in later works. An enumeration is like a logical partition. Suppose that we wish to investigate some group S of objects. We make an enumeration of S if, and only if, we "divide" S into some number of subclasses (categories)—say, P and Q—such that each member of S now belongs to exactly one of the subclasses, to either P or Q, and the union of P and Q will be S. The "division" can be done by applying what today is called an *equivalence relation* to the objects being investigated. Descartes refers to this as a *common nature* (see **Common Nature**). For example, suppose that we wanted to investigate a bunch of monochromatic marbles scattered about on the floor. Let this group of marbles be S. We can apply the equivalence relation "x has the same color as y" to the marbles on the floor, where by taking any two marbles a and b from the floor, if "a is the same color as b" is true, we place a and b in a jar. Marbles of the same color will be in the same jar. (The jars here are analogs to the subclasses P, Q, etc.) This will enumerate the marbles, for every marble will be in exactly one jar, and the union of the jars will be the original group of marbles S with which we began.

The investigative value of enumerating is great. As Descartes says, "by means of enumeration nothing will wholly escape us and we shall be seen to have some knowledge on every question" (AT X 388; CSM I 25). For "even though the object of our inquiry eludes us, provided we have made an enumeration we shall be wiser at least to the extent that we shall perceive that it could not possibly be discovered by any method known to us" (AT X 389; CSM I 26). So, even though the number of objects we wish to investigate is large (indefinitely so), if we establish an enumeration of these objects, investigating them is not only made possible, but manageable. This is so because the number of items we need to examine has been reduced. Consider, for instance, how a truth-table can reduce the number of items to be examined. There are an infinite number of natural language arguments, for example, that take the form of Modus Ponens. A natural language argument is *valid* if, and only if, the form it takes meets a specific criterion—the form will be such that there are no natural language arguments that take the form such that the premises are true and conclusion false. How might we determine whether a natural language argument that takes the form of Modus Ponens is valid? Well, we would need to determine that there are no natural language arguments that take this form such that their premises are true and conclusion false. But there are an infinite number of such arguments! In virtue of the number of natural language arguments to be examined, the objects of inquiry will no doubt elude us. A truth-table, which is akin to an enumeration, is a classification scheme that sorts all possible natural language arguments that take a particular argument form. Thus, the truth-table for Modus Ponens sorts all natural language arguments that take this form. As any beginning logician learns, there are only four categories in this table. Also, by examining the table, which requires us to look at only four possible cases, we can easily determine that no natural language argument that takes this form is such that it can have (all) true premises and a false conclusion. We can conclude with certainty, then, that any natural language argument that takes this form is valid. The enumeration turned an otherwise endless task into a manageable, easy one. It is not too far fetched to think that Descartes believed that such a method could be used in our investigations of bodies (like those marbles), especially given that their number far exceeded our ability to observe each and every object of inquiry.

Descartes's method specifically aims at enumerating what he calls *simple natures*. The simple natures are the constituents or elements of the contents of our ideas. *Extension* is a simple nature, as is *size* and *shape*. *Thought* is a simple nature, as is *color* and *sound* (these latter would later be called *sensible qualities*). For example, the content of the sensory idea of the Sun is constituted of simple natures—for instance, extension, size, shape, heat, yellow, and so on. Descartes analyzes the simple natures by applying the equivalence relation (common notion) "x modifies the same attribute as y." *Size* and *shape*, for instance, modify (are modes of) the same attribute, *extension*; *heat* and *yellow* modify (are modes of) *thought*. Extension and thought are what Descartes calls the *principal attributes*. So, let the group of simple natures be S. Also apply the equivalence relation "x modifies the same principle attribute as y." This will produce an enumeration of the simple natures. Each simple nature will be a member of exactly one of the new subclasses (*extension* or *thought*), and the union of these subclasses will be all the simple natures originally constituting S. We might call this enumeration—the enumeration that divides the simple natures into the mutually exclusive subclasses of extension and thought—the *master enumeration*. Secondary Source: Smith (2010b).

Essence (L. *essentia, naturam*; F. *essence, nature*). Traditionally understood, the essence of a thing is that which accounts for a thing's being the kind of thing it is. For example, the essence of a Euclidean triangle (*essentia trianguli*) is whatever properties a thing must possess in order to be this kind of geometrical figure, such that were any one of these properties removed, the thing in question would cease to be a Euclidean triangle (AT VII 64–5; CSM II 44–5). Descartes will many times identify the essence of a thing with its nature. Aside from geometrical essences, Descartes says that God has an essence (*essentia Dei*) (AT VII 66; CSM II 46). Even so, unlike his Aristotelian counterparts of the period, Descartes does not recognize essences that express the natures of natural kinds—for example, the nature of a tiger or the nature of an oak tree. Rather, other than the natures of geometrical figures and the nature of God, he recognizes only two, namely, the essence or nature of mind, which is to think (*cogitatio constituit naturam substantiæ cogitantis*), and the essence or nature of body, which is to be extended in length, breadth, and depth (*extensio in longum, latum & profundum, substantiæ corporeæ naturam constituit*) (AT VIIIA 25, 30–1; CSM I 210, 215).

Eternal Truths (L. *Æternas veritates*; F. *verité eternelle*). We find the conception of eternal truths early in Descartes's writings— for example, in *The World* (AT XI 47; CSM I 97). In the *Principles*, Descartes says that eternal truths have no existence outside our thought (AT VIIIA 22; CSM I 208). They are propositions (*propositio*) that are *not* things that exist independently of the mind (AT VIIIA 23–4; CSM I 209). The eternal truths are truths about the essential natures of things. For example, the eternal truth that the sum of the interior angles of a Euclidean triangle equal the sum to two right angles expresses the essence or nature of a Euclidean triangle. Even though they are not things that exist independently of the mind, the eternal truths do not *depend* on the human mind, but depend solely on God (AT VII 436; CSM II 294). The sense in which they depend on God is that God ordains them at the creation of the cosmos. Such truths did not exist "prior" to God's willing them. For instance, God did not will "that the three angles of a triangle should be equal to two right angles because he recognized that it could not be otherwise . . . On the contrary . . . it is because he willed that the three angles of a triangle should necessarily equal two right angles that this is true and cannot be otherwise" (AT VII 432; CSM II 291).

Evil genius (L. *genium malignum*; F. *mauvais genie*). This is sometimes translated "malicious demon." It is also translated "evil genius." The choice of "*genium*" (in Latin) or "*genie*" (in French) is telling. Both are derived from the ancient Greek word "*genesis*," which means origin, source, or birth—in short: *creation*. Descartes introduces the idea of the evil genius in the First Meditation. In this context, Descartes says that although he has always been under the impression that God was the creator of man and that the nature of God was such that doing evil was inconsistent with God's nature, he (Descartes) will assume the worse, and hold that not God but some evil genius created him. The aim of the evil genius is to deceive us whenever possible. The challenge, then, is to see whether we can discover any belief that is immune to the evil genius's power to deceive. In the First and Second Meditations, Descartes casts this "creator" not only as evil, but also as supremely powerful. By the end of the Third Meditation, and beginning of the Fourth, Descartes is able to argue that such a being is actually a logical contradiction. It is akin to a square–circle. So, the skeptical concerns that it allowed Descartes to raise in the First Meditation are shown to have been based on a contradiction, which allows Descartes in the Second Meditation onward to abandon those concerns.

Existence (L. *existentia*; F. *l'existence*). Descartes will sometimes cast existence as an attribute (AT VIIIA 26; CSM I 211–2). In this context, existence is understood as the *duration* of thing, presumably its duration over time. In other places, he goes the other way, defining *duration* in terms of *existing over time*: "[W]e should regard the duration of a thing simply as a mode under which we conceive the thing in so far as it continues to exist" (AT VIIIA 26; CSM I 211). He also will say, "since a substance cannot cease to endure without also ceasing to be, the distinction between the substance and its duration is merely a conceptual one" (AT VIIIA 30; CSM I 214). Thus, the extension of a body, which is the *what* of its being, is only conceptually distinct from this body's existence or duration over time. What this means is that existence is merely a way of conceiving a thing (a *being*, whether mind or body). This aligns with his casting existence as an attribute (for more, see **Distinction, Conceptual**; **Attribute**; and **Time**). In other contexts, however, Descartes seems to equate existence with the possession of formal reality. To say that a thing exists is to say that it possesses some level of formal reality (AT VII 102–3; CSM II 74–5).

Extension/Body (L. *extensa/corpus*; F. *extension/corps*). Descartes defines "body" in the Second Replies of the *Meditations* as follows: "The substance which is the immediate subject of local extension and of the accidents which presuppose extension, such as shape, position, local motion and so on, is called *body*" (AT VII 161; CSM II 114). Earlier in the Synopsis of the *Meditations*, he wrote, ". . . body, taken in the general sense, is a substance . . ." (AT VII 14; CSM II 10). Thus, body is an extended (or corporeal) substance. Even so, he will sometimes use "body" to refer to the *human* body (AT VII 14, 81; CSM II 10, 56). In the *Principles*, Descartes again asserts, ". . . extension in length, breadth, and depth constitutes the nature of corporeal substance" (AT VIIIA 25; CSM I 210). Also, again, he asserts, "Everything else which can be attributed to body [e.g., shape, size, motion, position] presupposes extension, and is merely a mode of an extended thing . . ." (*Ibid.*). Extension is the *principal* attribute of body (AT VIIIA 25; CSM I 210). Descartes argues, "if we perceive the presence of some attribute, we can infer that there must also be present an existing thing or substance to which it may be attributed" (AT VIIIA 25; CSM I 210). This line of reasoning is rooted in what he calls a *conceptual or rational distinction*. Such a distinction holds "between a substance and some attribute of that substance without which the substance is unintelligible" (AT VIIIA 30; CSM I 214) (for more, see **Attribute** and **Distinction, Conceptual**). The very conception of body requires that one conceive it as extended in length, breadth, and depth. Thus, one cannot conceive of corporeal *substance* minus its corporeality (its extendedness). It is important to understand that for Descartes a body is not something that is essentially solid, hard, or heavy. Body considered generally, he says, "consists not in its being something which is hard or heavy or [even] colored, or which affects the sense in any way, but simply in its being something which is extended in length, breadth and depth" (AT VIIIA 42; CSM I 224). What this suggests is that the "empty" space surrounding a hard (or solid) body, insofar as this space is extended in length, breadth, and depth, is as much a *body* or a *corporeal substance* as the hard body it surrounds. The material cosmos is thus a singular *plenum*. This has led to a disagreement among scholars as to whether Descartes held there to being only one body (or one corporeal substance), identified as *res extensa* (the extended thing), or a plurality of distinct bodies (or distinct corporeal substances) (for more on this, see **Distinction, Real**). Even so, all agree that Descartes refrains from claiming that the plenum, or the expanse of the material cosmos, is infinite. Rather, he claims that the plenum, or the expanse of the material cosmos, is indefinite (AT VIIIA 14–5; CSM I 201–2. For more see **Infinite**). Descartes also drew no essential distinction between "living" and "nonliving" bodies. The former are simply machines, complex arrangements of bodies (i.e., regions of extension) configured in certain ways (e.g., February 5, 1649 letter to More, AT V 277–8; CSMK III 366. See also **Animal** and **Soul**).

F

Faculty (L. *facultatum*; F. *faculté*). A faculty is a capacity. Descartes seems to adopt a Scholastic theory of mind, at least as that theory applied to human or finite minds, that claimed that there are two fundamental faculties or capacities of a mind: the (pure) *intellect* and the *will*. An embodied mind, says Descartes, gives rise to at least two additional faculties or capacities, namely, *imagination* and *sensation*. The faculty of the intellect is responsible for "producing" ideas. Ideas, on Descartes's view, are not, strictly speaking, images, but are *as it were* (*tanquam*) images of things (AT VII 37; CSM II 25). Ideas represent objects to the mind. Ideas are an essential constituent of every thought (*Ibid.*). But thoughts are more complex insofar as they also include as an essential constituent arising out of the faculty or capacity of the will. Descartes writes: "thus when I will, or am afraid, or affirm, or deny, there is always a particular thing which I take as the object of my thought, but my thought includes something more than the likeness of that thing. Some thoughts in this category are called volitions or emotions, while others are called judgments" (AT VII 37; CSM II 26). The view here seems to be as follows. Suppose that one eats a piece of chocolate cake. According Descartes's view, one is said to have been aware of the cake, made possible *via* an idea that represented it to the mind, where one is also said to have willed to eat the cake. The ideational element is accounted for by an appeal to the intellectual faculty, the will to eat is accounted for by an appeal to the volitional faculty. Here are two other examples, though they present subtle interpretative difficulties for Descartes. Suppose that one fears a lion. This can be explained as follows. One was aware of the lion by way of an idea that represented this object to the mind, where in addition one is said to have feared this object. Again, the ideational element is accounted for by an appeal to the intellectual faculty, the "fear" (here is where the subtle difficulties arise; for more on this, see **Emotions**) is accounted for by an appeal to the volitional faculty, the expression of the "fearing" relation being an active response (of one's will) to the object represented. Here is a less controversial example. Suppose that one affirms (the truth of) the Pythagorean Theorem. Again, the account goes as follows.

One was aware of the Pythagorean Theorem by way of an idea that represented it to the mind, where in addition one is said to have "affirmed" something about this object (for more on this, see **Judgment**). As in the other examples, the idea of the theorem can be accounted for by an appeal to the intellectual faculty, the "affirming" can be explained by an appeal to the volitional faculty. These three examples cover Descartes's list of volitions, emotions, and judgments. Secondary Sources: Easton (1997) and Lagerlund and Yrjonsurri (2002).

Falsity, Formal/ Material (L. *formalem falsitatem, formaliter falsa/falsitatem materialem, materialiter falsa*; F. *formelle fausseté/faussetté materielle*). Descartes first mentions formal falsity in the Third Meditation. It is, he says, falsity in the strict sense of the term. In this sense, it is a kind of falsity that "can occur only in judgments" (AT VII 43; CSM II 30). For example, were I to judge that the hat on the table is mine, and yet it turns out that it is not, then my judgment is false; it is formally false.

By contrast, material falsity "occurs in ideas," he says, "when they represent non-things as things" (AT VII 43; CSM II 30). His example of a materially false idea is the sensory idea of cold. Suppose that the idea represents cold as though it were a real or existent quality of, say, an ice cube (that one is holding in one's hand). Also, suppose that cold was really the absence of heat—that is, it was not anything at all. Then the idea that represents it as a real and positive (existent) quality of the ice cube is false; it is materially false. It represents a non-thing (i.e., a nonexistent quality in this case) as though it were a real thing (i.e., an existent quality).

Antoine Arnauld, in his objections to the *Meditations* (his is the Fourth Set of Objections), challenges Descartes's notion of material falsity. The gist of the challenge goes as follows: Descartes had claimed that the objective reality of an idea, the kind of reality it possesses in virtue of its representing an object, must have a cause. With respect to sensory ideas, the cause of the objective reality must possess a level of formal reality that is as great as the level of objective reality possessed by the idea; where the formal reality of a thing is the kind of reality the thing (the cause in this case) possesses in virtue of its being an existent thing. Thus, if the level of objective reality of an idea is that of a finite substance (i.e., it represents to the mind a finite substance), the level of formal reality of the cause must be at least that of a finite substance. Recall that Descartes had said that the materially false idea of cold is an idea that represents a nonexistent thing as though it were an existent thing. In this case, supposing that cold is really the absence of heat (i.e., it is not anything at all), and yet the sensory idea represented cold as though it were a positive (existent) quality of the ice cube, the idea would be materially false. Arnauld notes that since the idea *represents*, it must possess some level of objective reality. But the case assumes that cold is an absence (it is simply the absence of heat), in which case it lacks any level of formal reality. Arnauld concludes that the idea of cold would possess a level of objective reality that has no cause; it comes from nothing at all! This, Arnauld reminds Descartes, violates one of his most important principles, namely that something cannot come from nothing (AT VII 207; CSM II 146).

Descartes's reply to Arnauld is confusing, but some sense can be made of it. The gist of his reply is that the objective reality of the materially false idea of cold *does* have a cause, and so it does not come from nothing. The trouble, he says, arises from our wrongly taking a feature of the idea, the idea understood as the vehicle of representation, as the quality represented in the ice cube. This, of course, sounds as though the trouble arises as a result of a bad judgment, which if so, would be a case of formal falsity. Arnauld saw as much and at one point in his critique of the notion says that Descartes seems to have mistaken the falsity of an idea with the falsity of a judgment (AT VII 206; CSM II 145). Be that as it may, and rejecting this very point of Arnauld's criticism, Descartes again emphasizes that the *source* of such bad judgments is in the idea, where the idea provides subject matter for error in judgment (AT VII 235; CSM II 164). In other words, there is a falsity present prior to judgment, a kind of falsity *inherent* in some ideas. There is something inherently misleading in such ideas, independent of (and even prior to) judgment, and it is this inherent representational defect that Descartes calls *material falsity*.

Assume that the motions of the particles constituting the ice cube effect the motions of the particles constituting one's hand, which in turn effect the motions of the animal spirits filling one's interior brain cavity. The latter, Descartes says, can effect the surface of the pineal gland, and one result will be the occasioning of certain ideas in one's mind. Assume that one of the ideas occasioned in this case is what is being called the (sensory) idea of cold. Since the formal reality of the motions of the particles constituting the ice cube is the origin of the objective reality of this idea, there is an identifiable "cause" (or origin) of the objective reality contained in this idea. What is more, Descartes's view seems to be that in being the origin (as some scholars would put it, the *occasional cause*), the idea represents these motions, which metaphysically speaking are a mode of the body effecting the hand—here, this particular body is being called an *ice cube*. So, the (sensory) idea of cold represents a mode of a body (the ice cube). Descartes suggests in other places that with respect to the union (of mind and body), certain mental operations are disturbed (AT II 38; CSMK III 99, AT VII 375; CSM II 258). Presumably one of the operations that is disturbed is the operation of representation. Assume that the *cold* (the quality) that arises in the sensory idea is the "disturbance." This "disturbance" is that *by way of which* the idea is representing the mode of body (the motions of the particles constituting the ice cube in this case). The idea provides subject matter for error in judgment by presenting the *cold*, the mental quality (it is the disturbance of the mental operation of representation), instead of the object the idea actually represents, the motions. In other words, the idea presents the *cold* as though it were the quality of the ice cube being represented. As Descartes tells Arnauld: "For it often happens in the case of obscure and confused ideas—and the ideas of heat and cold fall into this category—that an idea is referred to something other than that of which it is in fact the idea" (AT VII 233; CSM II 163). Here, this might be read as telling us that despite the fact that the (sensory) idea of cold represents a mode of the ice cube (motions), in presenting as its "object" the *cold*, one can be led to think that the *cold*, this quality, is a mode of the ice cube.

So why does Descartes call this kind of falsity *material falsity*? He tells Arnauld that the term was borrowed from Francisco Suarez's *Metaphysical Disputations*, Part IX, Section 2, Number 4 (AT VII 235; CSM II 164). Even so, a close look at this text shows that Descartes is not really using the term as did Suarez. Although the

Preface to the *Meditations* was written after Arnauld had made his objections, Descartes introduces a distinction there that is of some interpretative help. He says that there are two ways of conceiving or regarding our ideas. The first is *materially*, when we regard an idea as an operation of the intellect. The second is *objectively*, when we regard the idea as the *content* it presents to the mind by way of this operation (AT VII 8; CSM II 7). Now, if when representing the motions of the particles constituting the ice cube the idea, here regarded as an operation of representation, is "disturbed" (because of the union of mind and body), where this "disturbance" is the presence of the quality *cold*, and it is by way of the *cold* that the motions are represented to the mind, we can see why Descartes may have referred to this kind of falsity in ideas a *material* falsity. The falsity arises directly from the idea regarded in terms of its being an operation of representation—that is, from the idea regarded *materially*. Hence the phrase "material falsity." Secondary Sources: Wilson (1978), Beyssade (1992), Field (1993), Wells (1984), Nelson (1996), and Smith (2005).

Force (L. *vis*; F. *force*). This has been a difficult concept for scholars to ferret out of Descartes's writings. Even so, he does say some things that help narrow down the notion of force. In Part Two, Articles 43 and 44 of the *Principles*, for example, he seems to cast force as a "tendency" or a "power" to continue to move in a direction (AT VIIIA 66–7; CSM I 243–4). Secondary Source: Slowik (2013).

Formal/Objective Reality (L. *realitatem formalem/realitatem objectivam*; F. *realité formelle*). This is an important distinction for Descartes's ontology. It also plays a crucial role in his theory of ideational representation. Let's look at these concepts one at a time.

The formal reality of a thing is the kind of reality the thing possesses in virtue of its being an *actual* or an *existent* thing (AT VII 103; CSM II 75). Since Pegasus is a nonexistent object, Pegasus is understood as lacking formal reality. The short of it is that to possess formal reality is to exist; it is to be an actual thing. Even so, possessing formal reality is not an all or nothing affair. There are at least three "levels" of formal reality: the level of an infinite substance, the level of a finite substance, and the level of a mode. The level of formal reality of an infinite substance is greater than that of a finite substance, and the level of formal reality of a finite substance is greater than that of a mode (AT VII 165; CSM II 117). There is an ontological relationship holding between the "objects" that inhabit these levels. The level of formal reality of an infinite substance is greater than that of a finite substance insofar as a finite substance depends for its formal being on the formal being of an infinite substance in a way that the formal being of an infinite substance does not depend for its being on the formal being of a finite substance. Likewise, the level of formal reality of a finite substance is greater than that of a mode insofar as a mode depends for its formal being on the formal being of a finite substance in a way that the formal being of a finite substance does not depend for its being on the formal being of a mode. In terms of existence, an infinite substance is understood to be greater in the sense that a finite substance depends for its existence on the existence of the infinite substance, while the existence of the infinite substance in no way depends on the existence of a finite substance. On Descartes's view, God is the only example of an infinite substance. Mind and body are each examples of a finite substance (AT VIIIA 24–5; CSM I 210).

Understanding and willing are among the various *modes* of mind; shape and motion are among the various *modes* of body. All mental modes presuppose the attribute thought; all corporeal modes presuppose the attribute extension (AT VIIIA 25; CSM I 210). This is another way of saying that the formal reality of a mode depends for its reality on the formal reality of a finite substance in a way that the formal reality of a finite substance does not depend for its formal reality on that of a mode. In terms of existence, a finite substance is understood to be greater than a mode in the sense that a mode depends for its existence on a finite substance in a way that the existence of the latter in no way depends on the existence of a mode.

By contrast, the objective reality of a thing is the kind of reality the thing possesses in virtue of its *representing* something. On Descartes's view only ideas will possess objective reality, and they will possess it by their very nature (AT VII 41–2; CSM II 28–9). In many instances, Descartes treats objective *reality* and objective *being* as coextensive. When perceiving or conceiving the Sun, Descartes says, the "object" presented directly to the mind, the Sun as represented in or by the idea, is not the formal Sun, the Sun existing in the Heavens. Rather, the presented "object" is an objective being, the objective Sun, and is a mental object. But a subtle difference between objective *reality* and *being* can be gleaned from the texts. For instance, the difference between one's idea of the Sun and the idea of the Moon will not be in terms of their objective *reality*, for both would presumably possess the same "level," namely that of a finite substance. Rather, the difference would be made in terms of the "objects" being presented in the respective ideas. So, it could be said that these ideas "contain" distinct objective *beings*.

It is important not to confuse "objective" in this context with today's (general) use of the term, where in the more contemporary sense to say that the Sun is objectively real is to assert that the Sun is an object that can (and does) exist independently of the subjective instances of perception—that is, the objective Sun in this contemporary sense is something like a mind-independent object. On Descartes's view, the latter, the mind-independent Sun, is what he refers to as the *formal* Sun (see *Being*). On Descartes's view, to say that the Sun is an objectively real object is to assert that it is an object of the mind, a mental object, an object being presented immediately to the mind by way of an idea. In this sense, the objective Sun does not (and cannot) exist independently of the subjective instances of perception (or mental representation more generally). This is so because ideas, in being modes of minds, cannot exist independently of minds. Secondary Sources: Kenny (1968), Wilson (1978), Chappell (1986), and Smith (2005, 2014).

Formal/Eminent. This distinction has a long history in philosophy. Descartes no doubt encountered it when studying Aquinas (though he would have encountered it in reading other works of the earlier medieval and scholastic periods). For Descartes, the distinction can be found hard at work, for instance, in his discussions of causation (AT VII 40–1; CSM II 28), ideational representation (generally) (AT VII 41–2; CSM II 28–9), and his idea of body or corporeal substance (specifically) (AT VII 44–5; CSM II 30–1), to name only three. Here is the gist of the distinction. Let's begin with how it is employed in his discussion about causation. Suppose that *a* is the cause of *b*'s possessing the property *P*, where it is true to say, "*b* is *P*." *a* is said to possess *P* formally if, and only if, (1) *a* causes *b* to possess *P* and (2) it is true to say "*a* is *P*." Let *a* be a fire (e.g., a campfire), *b* be water in a pot, and *P* be heat. As the pot of water sits over the campfire, the fire causes the water to be hot, where it is now true to say, "The water is hot." According to the earlier definition of "formal possession," the fire possesses heat formally, since (1) the fire causes the water to be hot and (2) it is true to say "The fire is hot." Now, return to the more general formulation in which *a* is said to be the cause of *b*'s possessing the property *P*, where it is true to say "*b* is *P*." *a* is said to possess *P* eminently if, and only if, (1) *a* causes *b* to possess *P* and (2) it is not true to say "*a* is *P*." This time let *a* be a fire (again, a campfire), *b* a hunk of wood, and *P* the property of being black. We say that the fire causes this hunk of wood to be black. In contrast to the previous case, in which it was true to say "The fire is hot," it will not be true to say "The fire is black." According to the earlier definition of "eminent possession," the fire is said to possess black (or blackness) eminently, since (1) the fire causes the wood to be black and (2) it is not true to say "The fire is black."

In the Third Meditation, Descartes introduces the concept of what he calls the *efficient and total cause*. An effect, he says, can only be brought about by such a cause, where each and every property this effect possesses (or expresses) must ultimately come from its cause. "For where, I ask, could the effect get its reality from, if not from the cause?" (AT VII 40; CSM II 28) This is supported, he later says, by the principle that something cannot come from nothing (AT VII 41; CSM II 29). Even so, he recognizes that the cause may not possess every property that the effect possesses, at least not literally. That is, it will not always be true to say that the cause possesses a property possessed by the effect. As should be clear from the earlier definitions, in such a case the cause would be said to possess the property *eminently*. Descartes provides an example. "A stone, for example, which previously did not exist, cannot begin to exist unless it is produced by something which contains, either formally or eminently everything to be found in the stone"

(AT VII 41; CSM II 28). This, he says, also holds for ideas. For, the idea of a stone "cannot exist in me unless it is put there by some cause which contains at least as much reality as I conceive to be in . . . the stone" (*Ibid.*).

Freedom (L. *libertatem*; F. *liberté*). Descartes's view on freedom of the will can be understood in terms of his faculty psychology. There are two fundamental faculties of mind: *intellect* and *will*. The intellect is cast as *passive* in this context, the will as *active*. As he introduces the matter in the Third Meditation, Descartes tells us that the intellect can be understood as presenting "objects" to the mind—the presenting is done *via* our ideas. Some of these ideas (or the "objects" presented) have their origin in things existing independently of the mind (such as material objects), while others have their origin in the will itself (the will "summons" the ideas). When one senses the heat of the fire next to which one is sitting, the sensory idea of heat appears to have its origin in the fire, or in something existing independently of the mind, since the idea comes before the mind even against one's will (AT VII 38; CSM II 26). Contrast this to the memory of one's feeling the heat of the fire. In this case, the idea (the memory) is understood as coming directly from the will's "wanting" to recall the event (of sitting next to the fire). In either case, as he tells us in the Fourth Meditation, the ideas, in addition to presenting their respective "objects," present to the mind a good or a truth, and the more clearly this good or truth is presented, the more strongly the idea compels the will to assent (either to pursue the good or to believe the truth). The less good or the less truth exhibited in the idea (or the less clearly they are presented), the less compelled the will, and when no recognizable good or truth is exhibited, the will is *indifferent* to the "object" presented by way of the idea (AT VII 56–8; CSM II 39–40). Some scholars have considered this to be more than just a little odd, for Descartes's view is that the more the will is determined or compelled to assent, the freer the will, and the less it is determined or compelled the less free it is. In a state of indifference, for instance, the will is exhibiting "the lowest grade of freedom" (AT VII 58; CSM II 40).

To Hobbes, Descartes says that if we consider simply our own experience, and do not consider our nature in light of the larger context in which God is said to determine the universe, we find that we are free (AT VII 191; CSM II 134). He later says something similar in the *Principles*, where our being free is among the most evident things we can know from experience, and should be "counted among the first and most common notions that are innate in us" (AT VIIIA 19; CSM I 205–6). To Mersenne, Descartes says that when the will is indifferent it is less free versus the will's being compelled to assent by being clear about the truth or good of a thing, in which case it is freer (AT VII 432–3; CSM II 291–9).

In private correspondence, Descartes reiterates his published view. Indifference is a defect, stemming from our finite intellect, and in this sense is rooted in a privation; it is not a positive perfection or aspect of the will (AT III 360; CSMK III 179, April 21, 1641 letter to Mersenne). Even so, as he says later to Mesland, this indifference is solely rooted in a lack of knowledge, for it is to be understood as manifesting in degrees, the more reasons we have for knowing something to be true or good, the less the indifference (AT IV 115–6; CSMK III 233, May 2, 1644 letter to Mesland).

G

Gassendi, Pierre (1592–1655). Gassendi was author of the Fifth Set of Objections to the *Meditations*. His Objections were voluminous, so much so that Descartes (sarcastically) refers to it as a book (AT VII 203; CSM II 269–70). He advocated for a form of Epicurean atomism, and is in part responsible for reintroducing this doctrine to the seventeenth century.

Geometry. This is a science about space and its properties—such as shape, size, relative position, and the like. The geometrical system that Descartes refers to when using the word "geometry" is Euclidean geometry. For Descartes, since space is simply a way of conceiving extension, it would be better (in coming to better understand Descartes's view) to think of geometry as a science concerned with *extension*, but more specifically with its *modes* (see, e.g., what he says to Gassendi: AT VII 381; CSM II 262).

God (L. *Deum*; F. *Dieu*). Although there is every reason to think that Descartes held traditional Catholic views about the God of the Old Testament, the God of his "system" is cast in less anthropomorphic terms: "By the word 'God' I understand a substance that is infinite, <eternal, immutable> independent, supremely intelligent, supremely powerful, and which created both myself and everything else . . ." (AT VII 45; CSM II 31). The concept of God plays a grounding role in Descartes's epistemology. An atheist, Descartes admits, can be clearly aware of certain truths—for example, mathematical truths. "But he cannot be certain that he is not being deceived on matters which seem to him to be very evident . . . So he will never be free of this doubt until he acknowledges that God exists" (AT VII 141; CSM II 101). As Descartes had argued in the First Meditation, one can doubt whether one's faculty of reason is reliable (AT VII 21; CSM II 14). If this doubt is not resolved, one cannot ever be absolutely certain that what seems absolutely certain to one is in fact true. Descartes famously demonstrates in the Third and Fourth Meditations (and again in the Fifth Meditation) that God exists and cannot be a deceiver (AT VII 49–51, 53–4; CSM II 33–5, 37–8). It is also shown that one's mind, which is a finite mind, along with its faculties, which includes the faculty of reason, has its origin in the infinite being, in God. Thus, one can rely on the certainty provided by the faculty of reason (i.e., one can claim to have knowledge) only if God exists, God cannot deceive, and one's faculty of reason has its origin in God. Insofar as the atheist denies the consequent of this conditional, it follows that the atheist cannot rely on the certainty provided by his faculty of reason. He cannot claim to have knowledge.

H

Heart (L. *cordis*). Descartes believed the heart to be akin to a furnace. When blood enters it, the heat of the heart causes the blood to become rarified, expanding in volume, which then is forced to exit the heart into the circulatory system (AT XI 202; CSM I 108, AT VI 51–3; CSM I 137–8). As the blood expands, the heart also expands. When the newly rarified blood leaves the heart, the heart contracts. This is why the heart appears to beat (AT XI 254; CSM I 322). In these discussions, Descartes contrasts his view with that of William Harvey (1578–1657), whose view appeared in *De Motu Cordis* (1628)—*Concerning the Motion of the Heart*. Harvey had (rightly) claimed that the heart is a pump.

Hobbes, Thomas (1588–1679). With respect to Descartes, Hobbes is author of the Third Set of Objections of the *Meditations*. Hobbes was living in Paris in the 1640s, having fled England because of civil war, which explains how it was that Mersenne was able to make the connection between him and Descartes. He is perhaps best known for having authored *Leviathan or The Matter, Forme and of a Commonwealth Ecclesiasticall and Civil*, published (originally in English) in 1651, typically referred to as *Leviathan*. Secondary Source: Duncan (2013).

I

Idea (L. *idea*; F. *idée*). Descartes's Latin term *idea* is actually borrowed from Greek, the word ιδεα (*idéa*). Typically, Latin translations of this Greek word used *species*. The Greek word *idéa* is a derivative of *eidein*, which is a term denoting an aspect of vision, and is close in meaning to the infinitive "to look at." Likewise, the Latin word *species* is a derivative of *specere*, which, not surprisingly, is a term denoting an aspect of vision, and is also close in meaning to the infinitive "to look at" (English gets *spectator* and *spectacle*, e.g., from the related *spectare*). Both *idéa* and *species* were words used by philosophers to denote what in Plato's ontology were known as the *Forms*. These were genuine substances of the cosmos. Descartes uses *idea* to denote modes of mind. In being cast as modes, where modes depend for their being on the being of the substances they modify, ideas are *not* substances. This is but one of many significant departures from Plato.

There are two sets of distinctions that Descartes applies to ideas. The first is what can be called the *Formal–Objective Reality* distinction, the second is what can be called the *Material–Objective* distinction. Let's consider them in this order. The Formal–Objective Reality distinction draws a distinction between the two kinds of "reality" an idea possesses: formal and objective reality (for more, see **Formal/Objective Reality**). Insofar as an idea exists, it possesses some level of formal reality. Since it is a "mode" of a substance (a mind), it possesses a level of formal reality of that of a mode. Descartes took there be three levels of formal reality: that of infinite substance, that of finite substance, and that of mode. According to this hierarchy, infinite substance is greater than finite substance, and finite substance is greater than mode. This is so because the very existence and being of a mode depends on the existence and being of a substance in a way that the latter does not depend on the former. Likewise, the very existence and being of a finite substance depends on the existence and being of the infinite being in a way that the latter does not depend on the former. "The nature of an idea," he says, "is such that of itself it requires no formal reality except what it derives from my thought, of which it is a mode" (AT VII 41; CSM II 28). So, "In so far as the ideas are <considered> simply <as> modes of thought, there is no recognizable inequality among them: they all appear to come from within me in the same fashion" (AT VII 40; CSM II 27–8). By contrast, objective reality is the reality an idea possesses insofar as it is a representation of something. They possess this kind of reality by their very nature (AT VII 42; CSM II 29). So "in so far as different ideas <are considered as images which> represent different things, it is clear that they differ widely" (AT VII 40; CSM II 27–8). Such differences, which will include differences in the "levels" of objective reality possessed (depending on whether the idea represents an infinite substance, a finite substance, or a mode), will also be understood in terms of the "objects" represented by or in our ideas. So there is a difference in this sense between the ideas of "a man, or a chimera, or the sky, or an angel, or God" (AT VII 37; CSM II 25).

The second distinction, the Material–Objective Distinction, is introduced in the Preface to the *Meditations*. There, Descartes draws a distinction between an idea as an *act* of representing and the idea as that *content* or *object* which is "produced" by this act, the object presented directly or immediately to the mind. An *idea* (or the term), he says, "can be taken materially, as an operation of the intellect, in which case it cannot be said to be more perfect than me" (AT VII 8; CSM II 7). "Alternatively, it can be taken objectively, as the thing represented by that operation; and this thing, even if it is not regarded as existing outside the intellect, can still, in virtue of its essence, be more perfect than myself" (*Ibid.*). This appears to simply be an alternative rendering of the Formal–Objective Reality Distinction, but it is not. The most telling difference between these two distinctions is that Descartes uses the Formal–Objective Reality Distinction primarily to trace the origin of the two kinds of reality possessed by ideas. With respect to their formal reality, the origin is the mind (the mind to which we attribute the idea), whereas with respect to their objective reality, the origin can be objects other than the mind. For example, as Descartes demonstrates in the Third Meditation, the objective reality possessed by his idea of God has its origin in the formal reality of God. So, this distinction focuses on *two* relations: the relation that the idea has to the mind (of which it is a mode) and the relation that the idea has to what it represents. By contrast, Descartes uses the Material–Objective distinction to relate an idea *qua* act to the idea, the very same idea, *qua* content. Here, this distinction focuses on only *one* relation: the relation that an idea *qua* act or operation has to the idea, the very same idea, *qua* content.

Ideas play a central role in Descartes's epistemology and metaphysics. He says, for instance, in a letter to Guillaume Gibieuf (1583–1650), "I am certain that I can have no knowledge of what is outside me except by means of the ideas I have within me . . ." where (when clear and distinct) ". . . whatever is to be found in these ideas is necessarily also to be in the things themselves" (AT III 474; CSMK III 201). This aligns with what Descartes had said in the Fifth Meditation (AT VII 65; CSM II 45).

In the Second Replies, Descartes says that by *idea* he means "the form of any given thought, immediate perception of which makes me aware (*conscius*) of the thought" (AT VII 160; CSM II 113). As was noted earlier, when an idea is considered in terms of its objective reality or being, we are considering it in terms of its representational content. This is also repeated in the Second Replies, where by an objective being "I mean the being of the thing which is represented by an idea, in so far as this exists in the idea" (AT VII 161; 113). Here, the "object" is said to be "in" the idea. This will not be the only place where Descartes speaks of ideational "containment." Ideas contain their objects—the objective beings (see, e.g., AT VII 46, 102–3; CSM II 31, 74–5). *Idea* is complicated when Descartes also focuses on the *origin* of what they contain. For instance, "the idea of heat, or of a stone, cannot exist in me unless it is put there by some cause which contains at least as much reality as I conceive to be in the heat or in the stone . . ." In more general terms, then, "in order for a given idea to contain such and such objective reality, it must surely derive it from some cause which contains at least as much formal reality as there is objective reality in the idea" (AT VII 41; CSM II 28–9).

Here is the complication: Is the idea of God *of* God because the idea *contains* the essence or nature of God (in representing God to the mind), or is the idea of God *of* God because its content has its *origin* in God? Perhaps it is both. This possibility seems to hold for what Descartes will call *primary ideas* (see the entry for **Idea, Primary**). But clearly we can have the idea of Pegasus, for instance, where this idea can be said to be *of* Pegasus in the sense that the idea *contains* the essence or nature of Pegasus (it represents a winged horse), but it cannot be *of* Pegasus in the sense that the idea's content has its *origin* in Pegasus. It cannot because there simply is no Pegasus existing independently of the mind. There is still much work to be done on Descartes's theory of ideas.

Descartes famously draws a distinction between three basic kinds of idea: *innate*, *adventitious*, and *factitious*. Let's take these one at a time.

Innate ideas. Initially, the examples Descartes gives of innate ideas are the ideas that represent to him what a thing is, what truth is, and what thought is. These ideas, he says, are "derive[d] simply from my own nature" (AT VII 38; CSM II 26). The idea of God, he argues, is also innate (AT VII 51; CSM II 35). Also, in his reply to Gassendi, author of the Fifth Set of Objections, and in his reply to critics of the Sixth Set of Objections, Descartes does more than to suggest that the idea of body (extended substance) is innate

(AT VII 382, 441; CSM II 262, 297). To Hobbes, in the Third Replies, Descartes says that by "innate" he simply meant that "we have within ourselves the faculty of summoning up the idea" (AT VII 189; CSM II 132), which he repeats in *Comments on a Certain Broadsheet* (AT VIIIB 357–8; CSM I 303–4). This suggests that the ideas are not "stored" or "housed" in one's mind, like so many marbles in a box, but instead that the very faculty of the mind that is responsible for producing ideas in the mind is capable of producing these ideas without immediate assistance from objects existing "outside" or independently of the mind.

Adventitious ideas. These ideas, he says, are produced in his mind directly by objects existing independently of his mind, where the "production" occurs by way of the senses (AT VII 37–9; CSM II 26–7). Examples of such ideas are produced when "hearing a noise, . . . or seeing the sun, or feeling the fire . . ." (*Ibid*.). In other contexts, Descartes will refer to such ideas as sensory ideas or sensations (see, e.g., AT VII 75, 436–7; CSM II 52, 294–5). These would later be cast as "external" sensations—that is, they represent objects, or events occurring, "outside" one's body. Other sensations are cast as "internal," insofar as they represent objects, or events occurring, "inside" one's body (AT VIIIA 316–7; CSM I 280–1). Examples of such ideas are the ideas of pain, hunger, thirst, and so on.

Factitious ideas. These are ideas made by the mind, their contents constructed from other ideas. The ideas of chimeras (including Pegasus) are examples of factitious ideas. Secondary Sources: Kenny (1968), Wilson (1978), Chappell (1986), Nelson (1997, 2008), and Smith (2013).

Idea, Adequate/Inadequate. When Descartes speaks of adequate and inadequate ideas, it is usually within the context of a discussion about our ideas of finite substances. Sometimes, he uses "complete" in place of "adequate" and "incomplete" in place of "inadequate" (see, e.g., the January 19, 1642 letter to Gibieuf, AT III 474–5; CSMK III 201–2). An inadequate idea of a substance is produced by way of abstraction (see the entry **Abstraction/Exclusion**). Let's say that in considering one's idea of the Sun, one focuses on the shape as depicted in the idea while ignoring the other features included in the idea's content (its color, size, extension, etc.). Here, one has produced an abstract idea—the idea of a shape. Now, supposed that one now takes this shape as a thing, that is, as a *substance*, capable of existing independently of other substances. To think of the shape in this way would be a mistake, Descartes says, since the shape, which is simply a mode, is *not* a substance (*Ibid.*). This idea of shape is an example of an *inadequate* idea of a substance. But when I understand the idea in such a way that (1) the shape, which is a mode, as being underwritten (made intelligible) by extension and (2) that extension as the principal attribute of corporeal substance, then I now have an *adequate* idea of a substance. Generally speaking, the conceptual structure of an adequate or complete idea of a substance is something like *mode-entailing–attribute-entailing existing substance*. This structure is brought to light in *Principles*, Part One, Articles 52 and 53. There, Descartes argues that when properly understood, shape presupposes (entails) extension (Article 53), and extension (an attribute) presupposes (entails) an existing substance (Article 52) (AT VIIIA 25; CSM I 210) Secondary Source: Smith (2010a, 2010b).

Idea, Primary. Primary ideas are introduced in the Third Meditation. Descartes says, "For just as the objective mode of being belongs to ideas by their very nature, so the formal mode of being belongs to the causes of ideas—or at least the first (*primis*) and most important ones—by *their* very nature" (AT VII 42; CSM II 29). He adds, "And although one idea may perhaps originate from another, there cannot be an infinite regress here; eventually one must reach a primary (*primam*) idea, the cause of which will be like an archetype which contains formally <and in fact> all the reality <or perfection> which is present only objectively <or representatively> in the idea" (*Ibid.*). Although unclear, Descartes seems to hold that his innate ideas of God, mind, and body (and maybe even the primitive notion of the union) are examples of primary ideas. It is worth noting that Descartes's primary ideas, ignoring the possibility that they are the innate ideas just mentioned, seem not only similar to what Hume would later refer to as *simple ideas*, but to what Hume would say about their relationship to the original *impressions* of which they are copies (see *A Treatise on Human Nature* (1739), Book I, Part I).

Imagination. Descartes speaks of the *corporeal imagination.* This, he says, is located in the brain. It is a genuine part of the body (AT X 414; CSM I 41–2, see also AT VII 161; CSM II 113). In early writings he casts imagination and sensation as "instruments of knowledge," noting that although truth and falsity can have their origin in these faculties (i.e., capacities), "there can be no truth or falsity in the strict sense except in the intellect alone" (AT X 396; CSM I 30). In the Sixth Meditation, Descartes compares and contrasts the imagination with the intellect. "When I imagine a triangle," he says, ". . . I do not merely understand that it is a figure bounded by three lines, but at the same time I also see the three lines with my mind's eye as if they were present before me; and this is what I call imagining. But if I want to think of a chiliagon, although I understand that it is a figure consisting of a thousand sides just as well as I understand the triangle to be a three-sided figure, I do not in the same way imagine the thousand sides or see them as if they were present before me" (AT VII 72; CSM II 50). We can produce in the imagination, he goes on to say, an "image" of the chiliagon, but he is clear to point out that this image will be only a "confused representation." This is so because the imagination can only be so clear. Once the shape in question has surpassed some number of sides, the "image" of a 1,000-sided figure, for instance, will appear no different from the "image" of a 1,001-sided figure. The difference between the former and latter is made only through the understanding (the intellect). The imagination, as with the senses, is, certainly in Descartes's more mature writings, cast as a genuine faculty (capacity) of the mind (AT VIIIA 7; CSM I 195). Even so, at least as that capacity requires body or extended substance (here, an image is taken to be essentially an *extended* image), it appears to be a capacity that emerges from the mind's being united to a body. Again, in the Sixth Meditation, for instance, he says, ". . . I consider that this power of imagining which is in me, differing as it does from the power of understanding, is not a necessary constituent of my own essence, that is, of the essence of my mind. For if I lacked it, I should undoubtedly remain the same individual as I now am; from which it seems to follow that it depends on something distinct from myself. And I can easily understand that, if there does not exist some body to which the mind is so joined that it can apply itself to contemplate it, . . . then it may possibly be this very body that enables me to imagine corporeal things" (AT VII 73; CSM II 51).

Immortality. Descartes announces in the Synopsis of the *Meditations* that he had provided in the *Meditations* enough for a reader to construct an argument proving the immortality of the soul, this despite the fact that he himself nowhere explicitly makes the argument in the book. The argument that he suggests is lurking seems to require two important claims. First, there is the claim that mind and body are *really distinct*. Two things A and B are said to be really distinct if, and only if, we can conceive of A completely independently of our conceiving B, and vice versa (for more, see the entry **Distinction, Real**). So, real distinction between mind and body are shown (e.g., in the Sixth Meditation) by showing how we can conceive of the nature of mind independently of our conceiving the nature of body, and vice versa. Secondly, there is the claim that *corruption* (one way to cease-to-be) occurs by way of division. Here, "division" is another way of describing the *decay* of something. Individuated bodies are divisible by their very nature (in virtue of their being extended). By contrast, minds are indivisible. This is so because minds are (essentially) not extended. "For we cannot conceive of half of a mind, we can always conceive of half of a body, however small . . ." (AT VII 13; CSM II 9). The suggestion is that minds cannot be corrupted because they cannot be divided. Of course, they cannot be divided because they are (essentially) not extended. This sort of argument, he says, is "enough to show that the decay of the body does not imply the destruction of the mind, and are hence enough to give mortals the hope of an after-life . . ." (AT VII 13; CSM II 10).

Infinite/Infinity. In the Third Meditation, Descartes claims to have an idea of the infinite—the idea of an infinite being. He notes something about typical grammatical cases of stems and negative prefixes, and denies that this sort of thing holds in the case of "infinite." The point is this: take the case of *"moral."* This is the positive stem. We can negate this by simply adding the prefix *"im,"* getting *"immoral,"* which means, of course, *not* moral. Here's another typical case: take *"possible."* This is the positive stem. We can negate this by again simply adding the prefix *"im,"* getting "*impossible*," which means not possible. But the relationship between "finite" and "infinite" is importantly different from the typical case. According to Descartes, the very conception of the finite presupposes a (prior) concept of infinity. *Infinity* is not the negation of the *finite* (unlike the way that *immoral* was the negation of *moral*!) (AT VII 45046; CSM II 31). An analysis of the idea of the finite reveals that there are "added" negative elements, that when added serve to limit the idea of the infinite. A close examination of the idea of one's own mind, as a finite thinking thing, reveals exactly this: "And when I consider the fact that . . . I am a thing that is incomplete and dependent, then there arises in me a clear and distinct idea of a being who is independent and complete, that is, an idea of God" (AT VII 53; CSM II 37). The philosophical move here is very similar to what we find in Descartes's discussions of his adequate (or complete) and inadequate (or incomplete) ideas of a substance (see **Idea**, **Adequate/Inadequate**). In the case of finite substance, the adequate or complete idea of a substance includes the conceptual structure: *mode-entailing–attribute-entailing existing substance*. But, as Descartes makes it clear in *Principles*, Part One, Articles 51 and 52, God is actually the only true substance, since God does not depend on anything else for his existence. The finite "substances" mind and body, insofar as they depend on God for their existence, are not substances in this sense. Rather, it is in a modified sense of "substance" that we can think of them as such. Their being substances is based on the fact that they are really distinct from one another (i.e., we can conceive their natures independently of one another, which establishes that they can exist independently of one another—for more, see **Distinction, Real**). But in the strict sense of "substance," the finite mind is not a substance. So, if the complete idea of a substance (in the strict sense) includes the structure, attribute-entailing existing substance, then one's complete idea will reveal that one's nature, namely thinking, which is also finite in scope, entails some substance, which is so since it depends on nothing for its existence, and this is the infinite substance, or God.

Innate. Usually, Descartes means by this that the item in question, in saying that it is innate, is inherent in something. Thus, there are certain *ideas*, he says, that are innate. The idea of God is the paradigm example of an innate idea (for more, see ***Ideas*: Innate**). But, in response to Hobbes, in the Third Set of Replies, Descartes says: ". . . when we say that an idea is innate in us, we do not mean that it is always there before us. This would mean that no idea was innate. We simply mean that we have within ourselves the faculty of summoning up the idea" (AT VII 189; CSM II 132). Here, the innateness of an idea is understood in terms of some inherent *capacity* to drum it up. Connected to this is a peculiar remark he makes in *Comments on a Certain Broadsheet*. There, in discussing the ideas of pains, colors, sounds, smells, and the like, which are usually cast by Descartes as sensory ideas (ideas having their origin in the senses), Descartes casts the ideas of colors, sounds, and so on, as nevertheless being innate (AT VIIIB 359; CSM I 304). Scholars have wondered whether this particular capacity, the capacity he mentions in *Comments on a Certain Broadsheet*, is a capacity that emerges from the mind's being essentially united to a body. So, the view is that Descartes takes this sort of capacity to lay dormant in disembodied minds, but is "activated" upon the mind's becoming an *embodied* mind. Secondary Source: Alanen (2009).

Intellect. There are two fundamental faculties of the mind, the intellect and the will. The intellect, he says, enables him "to perceive the ideas which are subjects for possible judgments . . ." (AT VII 56; CSM II 39). It is important to stress that the subjects of possible judgments are ideas. So, the intellect is that faculty of the mind that ultimately "produces" ideas. This will be so even in the case of sensory ideas. For although it will be true, according to Descartes, that the origin of the sensory ideas he has are in (material) objects that exist independently of his mind—so the origin of his sensory idea of heat may be the fire next to which he (his body) is sitting— the ideas that arise (e.g., the idea of heat) are not "produced" by the bodies or the sensory organs, but are "produced" by the intellect. But here, the ideas that arise in such cases do not present to the mind the motions as they occur in the body (AT VIIIB 358–9; CSM I 304). Rather, as he sits next to the fire, the sensory idea of heat will present the quality *heat*, and not the motions of the little particles constituting the fire. This is a longstanding view of Descartes's. In

Description of the Human Body, for example, he casts light in terms of a system of minute balls moving in straight lines. As they come into contact with our eyes, "we have sensory awareness of two kinds of motion which these balls have" (AT XI 256; CSM I 323). The first kind of motion is their moving in a straight line (toward the eye), the second is their moving (rotating) around their own centers (*Ibid.*). "If the speed at which they turn is much smaller than that of their rectilinear motion," he says, "the body from which they come appears *blue* to us; while if the turning speed is much greater than that of their rectilinear motion, the body appears *red* to us" (*Ibid.*). His view is that God has instituted the correlation between motions of bodies, the animal spirits in the brain, and the pineal gland, with certain ideas in the mind. Thus, upon there being certain motions in the brain, his mind, *via* the faculty of the intellect, will "produce" the idea of heat, or blue, or red, and so on. Such an idea is a sensory idea or adventitious idea, since its origin is in his sensory faculty, though the mind's ability to produce such ideas, and subsequently the ideas themselves, are innate (*Ibid.*).

In the Fourth Meditation, Descartes compares the two faculties—the intellect and the will. The latter, he says, is expressed in one's affirming or denying, pursuing or avoiding, and the like. In this sense, it would appear to be unlimited in scope (AT VII 57–8; CSM II 40). By contrast, the intellect (or understanding) is limited. This is an important sense in which a finite mind is *finite*. In some cases, when the intellect puts forward an idea for the mind to consider, the will is compelled, for example, to affirm its truth (AT VII 58–9; CSM II 41). This compulsion of will is characteristic of a clear and distinct idea (see **Clarity and Distinctness**). The will is not compelled by some "outside" force (i.e., a force independent of the mind). Rather, God has instituted the compulsion so that ". . . a great light in the intellect [is] followed by a great inclination in the will . . ." (*Ibid.*). But in some other cases (and this will be the majority of cases), the intellect puts up an idea and the will is not compelled. One's will can assent or affirm, but in doing so, one runs the risk of erring in judgment. This is in fact Descartes's account of the possibility of error in human beings, an account that shows that God is not ultimately responsible for the error. The possibility of human error in judgment, he says, is simply this: "the scope of the will is wider than that of the intellect; but instead of restricting it within the same limits, I extend its use to matters which I do not understand" (AT VII 58; CSM II 40).

Intuition. Early in his career, Descartes had claimed that there are only two ways of acquiring knowledge, namely, through intuition and through deduction. By intuition he meant "the conception of a clear and attentive mind," which left no room for doubt (AT X 368; CSM I 14). This evolves into what he would later refer to as clear and distinct perception (AT VII 35–6; CSM II 24–5). Earlier, when proposing intuition and deduction as means to acquiring knowledge, the former was considered to be a simple act of the mind, while the latter was considered to be a movement of the mind, moving from one thought to another. Since deduction was more complex of the two mental acts, and there was always the possibility of a wrong move, intuition was considered to be the salient mental act. Intuition in this context is not a psychological "hunch," as it might be said today. Also, intuition in this context is not identical with Kant's sense, Kant having used "intuition" to refer to an instance of sensory experience.

L

Language. In *The World*, Descartes says that words signify things. Human beings associate the sounds or written symbols with the things signified. The association between word and thing signified is a product of human convention (AT XI 4; CSM I 81). In a 1641 letter to Mersenne, he says, "Words are human inventions" (AT III 417; CSMK III 187). In the *Discourse*, he says that words are used to declare our thoughts to one another. The ability to use words to do this is what separates human beings from animals and machines (AT VI 56–7; CSM I 139–40). He says the same thing in a 1646 letter to the Marquess of Newcastle (AT IV 574; CSMK III 303), and again in a 1649 letter to Henry More (AT V 278; CSMK III 366). To Thomas Hobbes, Descartes says that the things signified by our words are things we "link" together when thinking. "As for the linking together that occurs when we reason, this is not a linking of names but of the things that are signified by the names . . ." (AT VII 178; CSM II 126). This suggests that the things signified are not things that exist *outside*, or *independently*, of thought. They are *in* thought—the things thought. In other words, the *contents* of thoughts (or ideas) are what our words signify. This suggests that the content of a thought (an idea) is the *meaning* of a word. "Who doubts," he says, "that a Frenchman and a German can reason about the same things, despite the fact that the words that they think of are completely different?" (AT VII 179; CSM II 126) Hobbes had cast reasoning as the linking together of words. But clearly the Frenchman and the German can *mean* the same thing—for example, both can say (and mean) that they are hungry—even though they use *different* words to say it. Here, the *word* is taken to be a conventionally selected *sound* (or written symbol) and the word's *meaning* is taken to be the thing signified, which here is the content of a thought (or idea). Descartes asks: "For if he [Hobbes] admits that the words signify something, why will he not allow that our reasoning deals with this something which is signified, rather than merely with the words?" (*Ibid.*). That the meanings of words, the things signified, are in *thought* (and not things in the world) is further suggested in Descartes's saying, ". . . for we see that magpies and parrots can utter words as we do, and yet they cannot speak as we do: that is, they cannot show that they are thinking what they are saying" (AT VI 57; CSM I 140).

Law of Nature. God creates the laws of nature (AT XI 34; CSM I 91, AT VI 41; CSM I 131). They are spatiotemporal expressions (or representations) of God's eternal and immutable will (AT VIIIA 61–2; CSM I 240–1).

M

Material/Objective. This distinction is first introduced by Descartes in the Preface To the Reader of the *Meditations* (AT VII 8; CSM II 7). Some scholars have taken this distinction to be identical to the Formal–Objective Reality distinction (see **Formal/Objective Reality**). But as we shall see, there is a difference between them.

In the Preface To the Reader, Descartes says that the term "idea" is ambiguous. It can refer to an idea as an act or operation of the intellect, or it can refer to the object (or content of the idea) represented to the mind by way of this act or operation (AT VII 8; CSM II 7). When we use the term to refer to the act or operation of the intellect, we take the idea *materially*. That is, we use "idea" in the *material* sense. By contrast, when we use the term to refer to the object or content of the idea, we take the idea *objectively*. We use "idea" in the *objective* sense. No doubt, the latter is identical to considering ideas in terms of their objective reality or being, which constitutes part of the Formal–Objective Reality distinction. When considering ideas materially, which is to take them as acts or operations of the mind, we are considering them in terms of their formal reality or being, the reality they possess in virtue of their being existent modes. This has led some scholars to think that the Material–Objective distinction is simply an alternative formulation of the Formal–Objective Reality distinction.

Arguably they are not identical distinctions. Here is just one difference. When applying the Formal–Objective Reality distinction to ideas, the aim is to trace the origin of each kind of reality. "The nature of an idea," Descartes says, "is such that of itself it requires no formal reality except what it derives from my thought, of which it is a mode" (AT VII 41; CSM II 28). So, the origin of the formal reality of an idea is the formal reality of a mind, of which the idea is a mode. "But in order for a given idea to contain such and such objectively reality," he says, "it must surely derive it from some cause which contains at least as much formal reality as there is objective reality in the idea" (*Ibid.*). Although the objective reality of some ideas may come from the objective reality of other ideas, "there cannot be an infinite regress here; eventually one must reach a primary idea, the cause of which will be like an archetype which contains formally <and in fact> all the reality <or perfection> which is present only objectively <or representatively> in the idea" (AT VII 42; CSM II 29). Such "primary ideas," as he calls them, are such that the origin of their objective reality is the formal reality of some object, that when not the mind will be an extra-mental object. Applying this distinction to the (innate) idea of God, Descartes gets the following. The origin of the formal reality of the idea is his mind, of which the idea is a mode. The origin of the objective reality of this idea, however, is the formal reality of God, an *actual* infinite substance. Notice that the Formal–Objective Reality distinction considers two relations. First, the relation that the idea has to the mind (of which it is a mode), and second, the relation that the idea has to some object, that when not the mind is some object existing independently of the mind. The Material–Objective distinction is different. It considers only *one* relation, namely, the relation holding between the idea considered *as act* and this very same idea considered *as content*. This is enough to show that the Formal–Objective Reality distinction and the Material–Objective distinction are not identical.

Mersenne, Marin (1588–1648). Friend of Descartes's, who was instrumental in getting the *Meditations* published. He was a member of the Order of Minims. He played an important role in soliciting and gathering objections. This collection of exchange, known as the "Objections and Replies," was appended to the *Meditations*.

Method. A method is a set of rules that, if followed, will lead one to the truth. Descartes recognizes two methods: *analysis* and *synthesis* (see the entry **Analysis/Synthesis**).

Mind/Soul (L. *mente/anima*; F. *esprit/l'ame*). Descartes identifies the mind with the soul. The mind has two basic (inherent) faculties or capacities, intellect and will (see **Faculty**, **Intellect**, and **Will**). The "embodied" mind, which is a mind existing in *union* with a body—the *human being*—has two additional (inherent) faculties: imagination and sensation. The essence or nature of the mind is to think (AT VIIIA 25; CSM I 210). Modes (or instances) of thinking include doubting, understanding, affirming, denying, willing, imagining, and sensing (AT VII 28; CSM II 19). In some contexts, Descartes identifies the *self*, the "I" of experience, as being essentially a mind, a thinking thing (AT VII 27–9; CSM II 18–9). However, in other contexts, he will cast the self as arising from the "combination of body and mind" (AT VII 81; CSM II 56).

Soul. As just noted, Descartes identifies the soul with the mind. This is in stark contrast to how the soul was understood in the Schools.

Descartes was fully aware of how *anima*, the Latin equivalent of the Greek word ψυκη (*psyche*), was used in the Schools. *Anima* was understood to be an organizing principle of matter. There were three "levels" of organization. The first level is that of a structure or pattern organized in such a way that this organism maintains itself over some period of time, where it takes matter from its surrounding environment, integrates some it into its structure, and expels unused matter back into the environment. Such a structure also is able to reproduce other organisms of its kind. This was typically referred to as the *vegetative* level. Plants are salient examples of this level. The second level of organization builds on the first, where the structure of the new organism introduces two dispositions or characteristics not found in the first-level organism—the dispositions to *move around* and to *sense*. This level was sometimes referred to as the *sensitive* level, and sometimes as the *animal* level. (Animals are "animated" or living things—the word "animation" is also a derivative of *anima*.) Not surprisingly, animals are salient examples of this second level of organization. The third level of organization builds on the second (which in turn had been built on the first), where the structure of the new organism introduces a new disposition or characteristic—the disposition to *reason* or to *think*. This level was sometimes referred to as the *rational* level. The human being was *the* example of an organism whose structure or pattern expressed all three levels of organization: vegetative, sensitive, and rational. Notice here that there is only *one* soul. Human beings are organized by the very same soul (*psyche*) as are animals and plants. The concept of the soul played an important role in ancient Greek accounts of *living* things. The unique aspect of a human being, then, was not the soul but the mind (*nous*) that was manifested at the third level of psychic organization. Socrates's *mind* (*nous*) was distinct from Plato's. Each emerges from distinct organized bodies. Thus, what distinguishes one mind from another isn't the soul, but is matter. As should be clear, on such Aristotelian accounts, since the third level of organization is "built" from the second and first levels, a failure at the first two levels of organization would entail a failure at the third. In other words, the human *mind* depended for its very existence on the existence of the (living) human body from which it emerged . What is more, the soul is not identical with the mind, but rather the mind arises as a result of the soul's organizing body. Descartes's view can be understood as parting ways with this sort of Aristotelian view.

In identifying the soul with the mind, the former no longer served Descartes in his account of "life." The "living" bodies of human and nonhuman animals were explained in terms of mechanics. "Living" bodies were simply machines, no different in nature from clocks and fountains (see **Animals**). Given the soul and the mind were identical for Descartes, it followed on his view that insofar as animals lack minds they also lack souls. Here, in line with canonical theological views, Descartes held that there are individual souls (since there are individual minds). Even so, his departure from Aristotelian views seems to have gone only so far. For, perhaps ironically, Descartes seems to have thought that what individuated human minds was the "individuated" bodies to which such minds were united.

Mode (L. *modus*; F. *mode*). According to Descartes's ontological hierarchy, modes occupy the lowest rung on the ladder. A shape, for example, is a mode of body; an idea is a mode of mind. A mode is a modification of a substance. Sometimes Descartes will say that *mode* refers to our thinking about substances in a certain way. "We employ the term mode," he says, "when we are thinking of a substance as being affected or modified . . ." (AT VIIIA 26; CSM I 211). Some scholars have argued that this puts pressure on the view that modes are *in*, or are actual modifications of, substances. For, arguably, *shape*, which refers to a mode, could be understood as referring to how one is thinking about a body (as shaped), in which case it would still be up in the air as to whether *shape* referred to anything, any quality, actually *in* the body in question. In the *Principles*, Descartes introduces a distinction based on his conception of mode, called a *modal distinction* (see **Distinction, Modal**). But for the most part, scholars hold that for Descartes modes were taken to be actual modifications of substances. Thus, shape is a mode of a body, and is not simply a way of regarding a body.

More, Henry (1614–87). English philosopher. He was a member of a group of philosophers at Cambridge called the *Cambridge Platonists*. He corresponded with Descartes. In 1659, he published some of this correspondence in a book titled *The Immortality of the Soul*. He also knew John Dury (1596–1680) and Samuel Hartlib (1600–62), both of whom visited Descartes in the Netherlands around 1634–5. Among More's more famous friends was the philosopher/poet John Milton (1608–74), author of *Paradise Lost* (1667).

Motion (L. *motus*; F. *mouvement*). In the ordinary sense of the term, Descartes says, motion is "the action by which a body travels from on place to another" (AT VIIIA 53; CSM I 233). But in the technical sense that he prefers, "motion is the transfer of one piece of matter, or one body, from the vicinity of the other bodies which are in immediate contact with it, and which are regarded as being at rest, to the vicinity of other bodies" (AT VIIIA 53; CSM I 233). This is more technical because it relies on his conceptions of place, both internal and external, and space (for these, see *Place*). It is perhaps important to keep in mind that Descartes rejected the view of atoms moving about in the void. The latter, void or space, was as much a corporeal substance (a body) as the individual corpuscles moving about. Since he conceived "space" as a plenum, bodies in motion, which move relative to one another, must move ultimately in circles (AT VIIIA 58; CSM I 237). The idea is that if body A moves, it moves to a new "place" relative to its initial "location," and takes the "place" just occupied by some other body, say body B. But then body B must move, which takes the "place" just occupied by some other body, body C. Since the material universe is not infinite, the displacement cannot go on to infinity. Thus, the "chain" of motion, constituted of bodies A, B, C, and so on, will be circular, where body A's leaving "open" its initial "place" is immediately taken by the last body in the circle, say body Z. The entire circle of motion, then, is constituted of bodies A through Z.

N

Natural Light. The natural light, or as it is sometimes called, "great light in the intellect" (AT VII 59; CSM II 41), the light of reason, is that faculty of the mind that allows the mind to "distinguish truth from falsehood" (AT VII 38; CSM II 28—this phrase was added in the French translation, see CSM II 27, fn. 1). Descartes often contrasts it to what *Nature has taught him* (see, e.g., AT VII 38; CSM II 26–7). When he says that "Nature has taught me," he means "that a spontaneous impulse leads me to believe it, not that its truth has been revealed to me by some natural light" (*Ibid.*). For example, as I sit next to the fire, I am spontaneously led to believe that the heat is in the fire. This is something that Nature teaches. But, when properly examined, the natural light reveals the truth of the matter. The heat isn't in the fire. Instead, the fire is a corporeal event, the swift motions of tiny particles that affect the motions of the particles constituting my body. Those motions are transmitted to my brain, by way of the animal spirits, and the idea of *heat* is occasioned in my mind. Here, the occasioning of this idea and not some other has been determined by God *via* divine institution (AT VII 80–3; CSM II 55–8). It is probably not too far fetched to think that the notion of Descartes's natural light has its origins, historically speaking, in the myth of Prometheus. The "fire" that Prometheus gives to human beings is arguably the light of reason (or Descartes's natural light).

P

Passion. In the *Passions of the Soul* (1649), Descartes develops a view of the passions. Although not perfectly clear, a passion is cast as a thought in the mind (or soul) that arises from specific motions in the brain (here, it is the motions of the fine particles constituting the animal spirits) (AT XI 349; CSM I 339). It is a passion insofar as the mind (or soul) is affected by the body, the body acting as agent. In being affected, the mind is passive (hence the use of "passion"). The passions serve a specific purpose, namely, "they dispose our soul to want the things which nature deems useful for us (as humans)" (AT XI 372; CSM I 349). In other places, Descartes says that the *effect* of the passions on the soul is that "they move and dispose the soul to want the things for which they prepare the body" (AT XI 359; CSM I 343). The view that the passions *move* a person to perform some action is no doubt related to their sometimes being later referred to as *emotions*. Love, for example, is a passion or emotion that compels us toward the object loved, while hate is a passion or emotion that compels us to move away from the object hated (AT XI 387; CSM I 356). Unlike our sensory ideas, passions presuppose in their makeup some reference to what is good or bad for the human being. They express what we might think of as a utilitarian-like value, what is good (and in many cases this will be experienced as a *pleasure*) is that which promotes the preservation of the union of mind and body (the human being), and what is bad (in many cases this will be experienced as a *pain*) is that which threatens the preservation of the union (see also **Emotion**). Secondary Sources: Blom (1979) and Rutherford (2013).

Place/Space/External Place/Internal Place (L. *locus/spatium/ locus externus/locus internus*; F. *lieu/espace/lieu exterieur/ lieu interieur*). Four terms are importantly related to place—*space*, *corporeal substance*, *internal place*, and *external place* (also see **Extension**). Each term refers to one and the same thing. Where they differ is with respect to their *senses*. Their senses are determined by the various ways in which we conceive the region of extension in question. Let's look at these one at a time.

Place. The place of a body is its position or location relative to other bodies (AT VIIIA 47–8; CSM I 229).

Space. Generally, Descartes takes space to be coextensive with extension in length, breadth, and depth (AT VIIIA 48; CSM I 229). "There is no real difference," Descartes writes, "between space and corporeal substance" (AT VIIIA 46; CSM I 227). The two are only conceptually distinct (see **Distinction**, **Rational** and **Conceptual**). Let body A be a stone brick, where in conceiving it thus we take it to be an example of a corporeal substance. Descartes instructs his reader in his analysis of the idea of body A (*qua* stone brick) to "leave out everything we know to be non-essential to the nature of body: we will first of all exclude hardness, since if the stone is melted or pulverized it will lose its hardness without thereby ceasing to be a body . . ." (*Ibid.*). By stripping away all other nonessential properties, such as color, heaviness, and other qualities like cold, "nothing remains in the idea of the stone except that it is something extended in length, breadth, and depth. Yet this is just what is comprised in the idea of space . . ." (AT VIIIA 46; CSM I 227–8). The difference between space and corporeal substance, as noted earlier, is the way in which we conceive body A.

Were we to remove body A from the wall, leaving a "hole" where body A used to be, "the same extension of the place where the stone used to be remains . . ." (AT VIIIA 46; CSM I 228). Of course, now this "hole" might be said to be "filled" with air or with water, and so on. So, one might claim that one corporeal substance, body A, had been replaced with another corporeal substance (in the form of air or water). This can misleadingly prompt one to then hold that the extension "left behind," which is now occupied by air, say, is a *different* extension (or a different corporeal substance). But it is not. It is the very same extension that was "there" when body A was said to occupy this place. The space left behind, after "removing" body A, where even if we took it to be now "filled" with "nothing" (i.e., it is not taken to be "filled" specifically with air, or with water, etc.), in being extended, is as much a corporeal substance as body A, the stone! (*Ibid.*). In fact, as some have argued, there is actually no change in corporeal substance upon the removal of the brick, but the *space* pre- and post-removal of body A is one and the same corporeal substance! This is so because the very nature of body is to be extended in length, breadth, and depth.

As Descartes will argue with respect to the impossibility of a vacuum (defined as an extended nothing), "nothingness cannot possess any extension" (AT VIIIA 50; CSM I 231). So, when we conceive of the space once occupied by body A to be "filled" with "nothing," we cannot really mean "nothing," or a "nonexistent something," but instead must mean that it is "filled," but as just noted, that which "fills" this space, whether it be air, water, and so on, is irrelevant to our considering its being "filled." In other words, we are focusing on this place's (or space's) extension and ignoring any specific qualities, such as hardness, color, heat, cold, and so on. Thus, the distinction between what "occupies" the space pre- and post-removal is modal, not real.

External Place. This, Descartes says, is to be understood as "the surface immediately surrounding what is in the place" (AT VIIIA 48; CSM I 229). Consider body A, which, in having any location at all, will be located relative to other bodies. The surface surrounding A, which "separates" body A from the other bodies (relative to which A is located), is what Descartes is referring to as *external place*. If we removed body A from this location, and nothing else was altered, this external place would remain—of course, "internal" to this external place would be something other than A.

Internal Place. This, Descartes says, "is exactly the same as space" (AT VIIIA 48; CSM I 229). Now, CSM points out that *internal place* was traditionally understood as referring to the space occupied by a body (CSM I, 227, fn. 1). Descartes get close to saying just this: ". . . with regard to place, we sometimes consider it as internal to the thing which is in the place in question . . ." (AT VIIIA 48; CSM I 229). So, where body A occupies some location relative to other bodies, and external place denotes the boundary or surface "separating" A from the other bodies surrounding it, *internal place* is that region within or internal to the surface, which is currently occupied by A. Secondary Sources: Garber (1992) and Slowik (2013).

Pineal Gland. This is a small gland located in the lower region of the center of the brain. The anatomical description is that the nerves of the body, which are tubules, all meet in the brain. Where they terminate, they form the interior surface of the brain, a small cavity located at the brain's center. The pineal gland inhabits this small cavity. According to Descartes, as the sensory organs are stimulated by the motions of bodies coming into contact with one's own (human) body, the nerves (the tubules) open and close, which alter the configuration of the interior surface of the brain (the open and closing of the nerve openings form new patterns on the interior surface of the brain, the wall of the cavity). The animal spirits, very fine particles, which occupy the interior cavity, exit the new openings, the patterns formed by their exit (which relate to the patterns formed on the interior wall) producing "images" on the surface of the pineal gland, as the animal spirits brush up against it. These "images" or "figures," as Descartes refers to them, are "ideas." At least this is his view in the early *Treatise on Man* (AT XI 176–7; CSM I 106). The surface of the gland, he says, is the *corporeal imagination*. In the *Passions of the Soul*, he says that the pineal gland is the "principal seat of the soul" (AT XI 351–3; CSM I 340). This is where the soul exercises its influence on the human body—more here than anywhere else (*Ibid.*). But what is more, this is where the body exercises its influence most on the soul. "I am convinced of this," Descartes writes, "by the observation that all the other parts of our brain are double, as also are all the organs of our external senses—eyes, ears, hands, and so on. But in so far as we have one simple thought about a given object at any one time, there must necessarily be some place where the two images coming through the two eyes, or the two impressions coming from a single object through the double organs of any other sense, can come together in a single image or impression before reaching the soul, so that they do not present to it two objects instead of one. We can easily understand that these images or other impressions are unified in this gland by means of the spirits which fill the cavity of the brain" (AT XI 353; CSM I 340).

Principal Attribute. See *Attribute*.

S

Sensation (L. *sensus*; F. *sentimens*). In the Sixth Replies Descartes introduces what he calls "three grades of sensory response" (AT VII 436; CSM II 294). The "first grade" sense of the term *sensation* refers to motions in the brain (and bodily organs). In this sense animals could be said to have sensations. The "second grade" sense of *sensation* refers to the ideas that the previously mentioned motions occasion. In this sense, animals cannot be said to have sensations. The "third grade" sense of *sensation* refers to judgments, where these judgments are also occasioned by the previously mentioned motions (*Ibid.*). Here, the judgments are those that compel us to believe that objects existing "outside" or existing independently of our minds are causing in us our sensations. In this sense of *sensation*, animals cannot be said to have them. The last two senses of the term, then, are reserved for human beings.

In the *Principles*, Descartes says that sensations are neither to be attributed to the body alone nor to the mind alone, but to the union of mind and body—to the human being (AT VIIIA 23; CSM I 209). This looks to be different from what he had said in the Sixth Replies. This has prompted some scholars to think that Descartes took sensations to be modes of a third kind of substance, which in this context would be the human being (the union), where the human being is understood as a kind of Aristotelian *hylomorphic* unity. Another view is that a sensation is a singular mode that "straddles" both a mind and a body, where here the mind and body need not form a *hylomorphic* unity, or third kind of substance. Also yet another view takes a sensation to be a complex of modes, the complex constituted of a motion, which is a mode of body, and an idea, which is a mode of mind. Secondary Sources: Hoffman (1986, 1990) and Smith (2005b).

Simple Nature. Descartes says that simple natures are either "spiritual" (mental) or "corporeal" (bodily) (AT X 399; CSM I 32). They are the elements that constitute all objects of knowledge. *Volition* and *intellect* are simple natures that are associated with the mental, while *extension* and *shape* are simple natures that are associated with the corporeal (AT X 418–20; CSM I 44–5). There are simple natures that are "common" to both mind and body, namely *existence*, *unity*, and *duration* (*Ibid.*). Descartes sometimes casts simple natures as inhabitants of our ideas. They are what the mind directly perceives in any moment of cognition. Secondary Sources: Marion (1992) and Smith (2005b, 2010).

Skepticism/Doubt. Skepticism is a doctrine that claims that knowledge is impossible. Historically, there have been various "schools" of skepticism. Descartes identifies several from the ancient period: Pyrrho (or the Pyrrhonists), Epicurus, and so on. Descartes is not a skeptic, but uses skepticism to initiate his search for a foundation on which to build a *scientia*, a systematic body of knowledge. In the First Meditation, Descartes implies that to doubt a belief we must be able to conceive of a situation in which the belief is false. To put this more strongly, where *p* is a belief: *p* can be doubted if, and only if, we can conceive a situation in which *p* is false. According to this definition, if we cannot conceive a situation in which a belief is false, then we cannot doubt this belief. This is in turn importantly connected to Descartes's search for a foundation belief—a belief that cannot be doubted. This is directly related to Descartes's claiming that "I am thinking, therefore I exist" is foundational (see the entry **Cogito ergo sum**). For, as he argues, when considering the fact that he is thinking, he cannot conceive a situation in which he was thinking yet did not exist (while thinking). "I must finally conclude," he says, "that this proposition, *I am, I exist*, is necessarily true whenever it is put forward by me or conceived in my mind" (AT VII 25; CSM II 17).

Space. See **Place** and **Extension**.

Substance (L. *substantia*; F. *substance*). The term *substance* has two important senses for Descartes. Strictly speaking, a substance "exists in such a way as to depend on no other thing for its existence" (AT VIIIA 24; CSM I 210). This was a standard Scholastic definition of *substance*, traceable to Aristotle. For Descartes, the only thing that actually met this criterion was God (AT VIIIA 24; CSM I 210). Even so, Descartes uses the term to refer to the two kinds of "created" thing: *mind* and *body*. Of course, since they are created by God, and so depend on God for their existence, they are not substances in the strict sense. As Descartes will show, mind and body are *really distinct* (for more, see **Distinction, Real**). This entails that each can be conceived independently of one another, which entails that each can exist independently of the other. What is more, modes (such a shape or an idea) will depend on these two things (shape will depend for its existence on extension [body], while an idea will depend for its existence on thought [mind]). In this qualified sense, then, the term *substance* can apply to mind and body.

T

Thought (L. *cogitationes*; F. *pensée*). Thought or thinking is the principal attribute of mind. All modes of a mind, in fact, are understood in terms of thought. *Doubting, understanding, affirming, denying, desiring, willing,* to list several items, are all understood as various kinds of thought (AT VII 28; CSM II 19). In the Third Meditation, Descartes tells us that thoughts can be divided into various kinds. But here he divides them into simple and complex thoughts. The simplest kind of thought is an *idea*, which, he says, represents (or presents) an object to the mind. Ideas are *as it were* (*tanquam*) images of things (AT VII 37; CSM II 25). Other thoughts include an additional feature (in addition to an idea). These are the complex thoughts, where he lists willing, fearing, affirming, and denying, as examples

(AT VII 37; CSM II 26). Such thoughts include an idea, which exhibits to the mind an "object" (or some likeness of the object), where the "additional feature" is, for instance, the act of affirming. So, suppose that one has an idea of the Pythagorean Theorem. Presumably, the complex thought arises when one affirms the theorem (the "object" presented *via* the idea). The idea comes about *via* the faculty of the intellect and the affirming action comes about *via* the faculty of the will. Together the faculties of intellect and will work to produce a complex thought.

In the Second Replies, Descartes says that he uses the term *thought* to include "everything that is within us in such a way that we are immediately aware of it" (AT VII 160; CSM II 113). This is consistent with what he says about thoughts generally (whether simple or complex). This suggests, in addition to thought's being cast as the essential attribute of a mind, that thought is that by way of which the mind is made *aware of* things (see the entry for **Conscience/Conscious**).

Time (L. *tempus*; F. *temps*). Descartes says that some attributes are in things, others only in thought (AT VIIIA 26–7; CSM I 212). The duration of a thing is only conceptually distinct from its being. Thus, the duration of body is only conceptually distinct from its being extended (AT VIIIA 30; CSM I 214). Both extension and duration in this context seem to be examples of attributes that are in the thing. Now, when bodies are in motion, and we wish to measure their motion, we do this by considering or focusing on (in thought) the duration of their motion. We can compare the duration of their motion (so conceived) "with the duration of the greatest and most regular motions which give rise to years and days, and we call this duration 'time'" (AT VIIIA 27; CSM I 212). Here, the greatest and most regular motions he mentions are the motion of the Earth orbiting around the Sun (the year) and the motion of the circumference of the Earth rotating around the Earth's center (the day). Understood this way, "when time is distinguished from duration taken in the general sense and called the measure of movement, it is simply a mode of thought" (*Ibid.*). Time, then, looks to be an example of an attribute that is not in the thing, but in thought. Secondary Sources: Gorham (2007) and Slowik (2013).

Transubstantiation/Eucharist. The Eucharist, or Holy Communion, is a sacred rite in Christianity. The rite is based on the Biblical story of the Last Supper. The word "Eucharist" is sometimes also used to refer to the body and blood of Jesus, which are present when this rite is being performed, after the bread and wine (which become the body and blood) have been consecrated. Several Catholic and Protestant readers of Descartes expressed concerns over how Descartes's metaphysics conflicted with the Eucharist, the criticisms typically centering round the issue of transubstantiation. Arnauld, for example, author of the Fourth Set of Objections, predicts that Descartes's metaphysics will upset the theologians. "We believe on faith," he says, "that the substance of the bread is taken away from the bread of the Eucharist and only the accidents remain" (AT VII 217; CSM II 153). But Descartes's metaphysics holds that there are only two kinds of substances, namely *mind* and *body*, whose essences are *thought* and *extension*, respectively (see **Attribute**). He does not recognize what are typically referred to as "natural kinds." So, there is no *essential* difference between a star, the Earth, the Moon, water, air, a tiger, a human body, or a piece of bread. Each one, in being corporeal, is essentially extended—period. As Arnauld indicates, the theological view is that the underlying "substance" of the bread at the moment of consecration is "taken away," where it is replaced with another, namely with the "substance" of the body of Christ. This is what is meant by *transubstantiation*—there is a change with respect to the substance or substrate; one is being "swapped out" for another. But, according to Descartes's metaphysics, in being corporeal, there is no essential or substantial difference between the bread and the body of Christ. There is only the "swapping out" of extension with extension. So, the import of the replacement is rendered meaningless. Descartes's replies to these criticisms seemed to have only tossed him from the proverbial frying pan into the fire.

True and Immutable Nature. Descartes notes that there are things that we can think about, even at will, and because of this may appear to be completely dependent on the mind. But a closer inspection of these things shows that there are truths about them that are so independently of the mind (AT VII 64; CSM II 44). Consider the nature of a triangle. By considering this nature, we can demonstrate that the triangle has certain properties, as "its three angles are equal to two right angles" (AT VII 64; CSM II 45). This, he says, he recognizes "whether I want to or not . . ." and so "were not invented by me" (*Ibid.*). Descartes's view seems to be that the true and immutable natures are what they are due to God's willing them to be so (see also **Eternal Truths**). Secondary Sources: Nolan (1997a, 1997b).

U

Understanding, the (L. *intellectus*, *intellectionem*; F. [*faculté de*] *conseuoir*). The understanding was considered a faculty or capacity of the mind (see **Faculty**, **Intellect**, and **Mind**). Descartes treats the understanding and the intellect as coextensive. One faculty to which Descartes contrasts the understanding is the will. The scope of the latter is greater than that of the former. As a result, we can affirm things that we do not understand. This, he argues in the Fourth Meditation, is the origin of human error (AT VII 58–9; CSM II 40–1). Another faculty to which he contrasts the (pure) understanding is the imagination. This contrast is made, for instance, in the Sixth Meditation. An interesting difference worth noting is that whereas the understanding is an essential faculty of the mind, the imagination is not (AT VII 72–3; CSM II 50–1). The latter emerges as a faculty of an "embodied" mind—a mind that is essentially united to a body (see *Union* and *Mind/Soul*).

Union (L. *unione*; F. *union*). This term refers to the relation that holds between a mind and body. Descartes sometimes casts this relation as a union of mind and body, where the two "form a unit," the suggestion being that the two things become one, while at other times—and, in fact, in many of the very same discussions—casting it as an intermingling of mind and body, which suggests that the two things remain distinct and are not in fact a singular thing (AT VII 81; CSM II 56, AT VIIIA 23; CSM I 209). In his reply to Arnauld (Fourth

Replies), Descartes recasts his discussion in the Sixth Meditation as having established that "the mind is substantially united to the body" (AT VII 228; CSM II 160). Also, in the *Principles* he says that God has joined the two so closely that they are "compounded" (the word he uses is *conflavisse*, which comes from *conflare*, and means *to forge* or *to melt*) into a unity. But here, he immediately qualifies this by claiming that though forged into one, they "remain really distinct" (AT VIIIA 29; CSM I 213). Some scholars, in light of certain texts, have read such passages as telling us that the union is something like an Aristotelian *hylomorphic* unity. Others, in light of certain other texts, have read the same passages as telling us that the interaction *between* mind and body, and more specifically the "rules" that frame the very possibility of this interaction, constitutes the union, these "rules" instituted by God. This latter sort of reading allows mind and body to remain distinct while the union emerges in (or *as*) their interaction. Secondary Sources: Hoffman (1986) and Rutherford (2013).

V

Vacuum (L. *vacuum*). This philosophical term, Descartes claims, denotes an *extended nothing* (AT VIIIA 49; CSM I 229–30). An extended nothing, he argues, is a contradiction. A thing's "being extended in length, breadth and depth in itself warrants the conclusion that it is a substance . . ." (*Ibid.*). For, "nothingness possesses no attributes . . . Thus, if we perceive the presence of some attribute, we can infer that there must also be present an existing thing or substance to which it may be attributed" (AT VIIIA 25; CSM I 210). Extension is an attribute. But, "nothingness cannot possess any extension" (AT VIIIA 50; CSM I 231). Therefore, if there is an instance of extension, there must be some thing or substance that possesses this extension. Since this is so, there cannot ever be an extended nothing. In other words, a vacuum is impossible (*Ibid.*). Secondary Sources: Garber (1992) and Slowik (2013).

W

Will. The will is a faculty of the mind (see **Faculty** and **Mind/Soul**). The mind has two essential faculties: intellect and will. The intellect is a passive faculty, he says, while the will is active. The will is responsible for making judgments. "It is only the will," he says, ". . . which I experience within me to be so great that the idea of any greater faculty is beyond my grasp; so much so that it is above all in virtue of the will that I understand myself to bear in some way the image and likeness of God" (AT VII 57; CSM II 40) (see also **Freedom**). The will and intellect work together as follows. Something is presented to the mind *via* the intellect, and the will either affirms or denies (or pursues or avoids) what is presented (AT VII 57–8; CSM II 40).

Bibliography

Ablondi, Fred. "Geraud de Cordemoy," *The Stanford Encyclopedia of Philosophy* (Summer 2010 Edition), edited by Edward N. Zalta. URL = <http://plato.stanford.edu/archives/sum2010/entries/cordemoy/>.

Adamson, Robert. *The Development of Modern Philosophy*, edited by William R. Sorely. London: William Blackwood & Sons, 1930.

Alanen, Lilli. "Sensory Ideas, Objective Reality, And Material Falsity," *Reason, Will, and Sensation*, edited by John Cottingham. Oxford: Clarendon Press, 1994.

—. *Descartes's Concept of Mind*. Cambridge, MA: Harvard University Press, 2009.

Allison, Henry. *Kant's Transcendental Idealism*. New Haven, NY: Yale University Press, 1983.

Almog, Joseph. *What Am I?: Descartes and the Mind–Body Problem*. Oxford: Oxford University Press, 2002.

—. *Cogito?: Descartes and Thinking the World*. Oxford: Oxford University Press, 2008.

Aquila, Richard. "The Content Of Cartesian Sensation And The Intermingling Of Mind And Body," *History of Philosophy Quarterly*, 12:2 (April 1995) 209–26.

Aquinas, Thomas, Saint. *The Summa Theologica: Introduction to St. Thomas Aquinas*, edited by Anton Pegis. New York: Random House, 1945.

—. *St. Thomas Aquinas: Philosophical Texts*, translated by Thomas Gilby. New York: Oxford University Press, 1960.

Ariew, Roger and Grene, Marjorie. "Ideas, In and Before Descartes," *Journal of the History of Ideas*, 56 (1995), 87–106.

Aristotle. *Analytica Posteriora* in *The Works of Aristotle*, vol. I, edited by W. D. Ross, translated by E. M. Edghill. Oxford: Oxford University Press, 1928a.

—. *Categoriae* in *The Works of Aristotle*, vol. I, edited by W. D. Ross, translated by E. M. Edghill. Oxford: Oxford University Press, 1928b.

—. *Topica* in *The Works of Aristotle*, vol. I, edited by W. D. Ross, translated by E. M. Edghill. Oxford: Oxford University Press, 1928c.

—. *De Anima, The Works of Aristotle*, translated by J. A. Smith, edited by W. D. Ross. Oxford: Clarendon Press, 1931.

—. *Categories, A New Aristotle Reader*, translated by J. L. Ackrill, Princeton, NJ: Princeton University Press, 1987a.
—. *On Generation and Corruption, A New Aristotle Reader*, translated by J. L. Ackrill. Princeton, NJ: Princeton University Press, 1987b.
—. *Topics, A New Aristotle Reader*, translated by J. L. Ackrill. Princeton, NJ: Princeton University Press, 1987c.
—. *Nicomachean Ethics, Aristotle XIX* (Loeb), translated by H. Rackham. Cambridge, MA: Harvard University Press, 1990.
—. *Posterior Analytics*, translated by Jonathan Barnes, second edition. Oxford: Clarendon Press, 1994.
Arnauld, Antoine. *On True and False Ideas*, translated by Stephen Gaukroger. New York: Manchester University Press, 1990.
Arnauld, Antoine and Nicole, Pierre. *The Art of Thinking: Port-Royal Logic*, translated by James Dickoff and Patricia James. Indianapolis, IN: The Bobbs Merrill Company, 1964.
Ashworth, E. J. "Descartes' Theory of Clear and Distinct Ideas," *Cartesian Studies*. Oxford: Basil Blackwell, 1972.
Augustine (Augustinus, Aurelius, Saint, Bp. of Hippo). *De Dialectica*, translated by Darrell Jackson, edited by Jan Pinborg. Boston, MA: D. Reidel Publishing Company, 1975.
—. *De Ordine*, translated by Silvano Borruso. South Bend: St. Augustine's Press, 2007.
Baker, Gordon and Morris, Katherine. *Descartes' Dualism*. New York: Routledge, 1996.
Beck, L. J. *The Metaphysics of Descartes*. Oxford: Clarendon Press, 1965.
Berkeley, George. *Three Dialogues Between Hylas and Philonous*, edited by Robert Adams. Indianapolis, IN: Hackett Publishing, 1979.
Beyssade, Jean-Marie, "Descartes on Material Falsity," *Minds, Ideas, and Objects*, vol. 2, edited by Phillip D. Cummins and Guenter Zoeller. Atascadero: North American Kant Society Studies in Philosophy, 1992.
Blom, John. *Descartes: His Moral Philosophy and Psychology*. New York: New York University Press, 1979.
Boas, Marie. *The Scientific Renaissance 1450–1630*. New York: Harper & Row, 1962.
Bolton, Martha. "Confused And Obscure Ideas of Sense," *Essays On Descartes' Meditations*, edited by Amelie Oksenberg Rorty. Berkeley, CA: University of California Press, 1986.
Bos, Henk J. M. *Redefining Geometrical Exactness*. New York: Springer, 2000.
Boyer, Carl. *A History of Mathematics*. Princeton, NJ: Princeton University Press, 1985.
Buroker, Jill Vance. "Descartes on Sensible Qualities," *The Journal of the History of Philosophy*, XXIX:4 (1991), 585–611.

Chappell, Vere. "The Theory of Ideas," *Essays on Descartes' Meditations*, edited by Amelie Oksenberg Rorty. Berkeley, CA: University of California Press, 1986.
Chomsky, Noam. *Cartesian Linguistics*. New York: Harper & Row, 1966.
Clarke, Desmond. *Descartes' Philosophy of Science*. State College, PA: Pennsylvania State University Press, 1982.
Clatterbaugh, Kenneth. "Descartes' Causal Likeness Principle," *Philosophical Review*, 89:3 (July 1980), 379–402.
Collins, James. "Descartes' Philosophy of Nature," in *American Philosophical Quarterly*, monograph series (monograph no. 5), edited by Nicholas Rescher. Oxford: Basil Blackwell, 1971.
Cottingham, John. "Descartes on Colour," *Proceedings of the Aristotelian Society*, New Series, 90 (1989–90), 231–46.
Cress, Donald A. "Truth, Error, and the Order of Reasons," *Reason, Will, and Sensation*, edited by John Cottingham. Oxford: Clarendon Press, 1994.
Crombie, A. C. *Augustine to Galileo*, 2 vols. Cambridge, MA: Harvard University Press, 1961.
Cunning, David and Nelson, Alan. "Cognition and Modality in Descartes," *Acta Philosophica Fennica*, 64 (1999), 137–53.
—. "Descartes on the Dubitability of the Existence of Self," *Philosophy and Phenomenological Research*, 74:1 (2007), 111–31.
Curley, Edwin. *Descartes Against the Skeptics*. Cambridge, MA: Harvard University Press, 1978.
Curley, E. M. "Spinoza as an expositor of Descartes," in *Speculum Spinozanum*, edited by S. Hessing. London: Routledge & Kegan Paul, 1977, pp. 133–42.
—. "Analysis in the Meditations: The Quest for Clear and Distinct Ideas," in *Essays on Descartes' Meditations*, edited by Amelie Oksenberg Rorty. Berkeley, CA: University of California Press, 1986.
Descartes, Rene. *The Geometry of Descartes*, translated by Eugene Smith and Marcia Latham. New York: Dover Publications, 1954.
—. *Philosophical Letters*, translated by Kenny. Oxford: Clarendon Press, 1970.
—. *Oeuvres De Descartes*, The Adam and Tannery volumes (AT), 11 vols. Paris: Librairie Philosophique J. Vrin, 1983.
—. *The Philosophical Writings of Descartes*, Cottingham, Stoothoff, and Murdoch translations (CSM), 3 vols. Cambridge: Cambridge University Press, 1988.
Descartes' Conversation with Burman, translated by John Cottingham. Oxford: Clarendon Press, 1976.
De Wulf, Maurice. *Scholastic Philosophy*, translated by P. Coffey. New York: Dover Publications, 1956.
Des Chene, Dennis. *Physiologia: Natural Philosophy in Late Aristotelian and Cartesian Thought*. Ithaca, NY: Cornell University Press, 2000.

Dod, Bernard. "Aristotles Latinus," *The Cambridge History of Later Medieval Philosophy*, edited by Norman Kretzmann, Anthony Kenny, and Jan Pinborg. Cambridge: Cambridge University Press, 1982.
Duncan, Stewart, "Thomas Hobbes," *The Stanford Encyclopedia of Philosophy* (Summer 2013 Edition), edited by Edward N. Zalta. URL = <http://plato.stanford.edu/archives/sum2013/entries/hobbes/>.
Durant, Will. *The Story of Philosophy*. Garden City: Garden City Publication Co., 1943.
Easton, Patricia (ed). *Logic and the Workings of the Mind*, vol. 5 of the series North American Kant Society Studies in Philosophy. Atascadero, CA: Ridgeview Publishing, 1997.
Evans, G. R. *Philosophy and Theology in the Middle Ages*. New York: Taylor & Francis, 2003.
Field, Richard W. "Descartes' Proof of the Existence of Matter," *Mind* (New Series), 94:374 (April 1985), 244–49.
—. "Descartes on the Material Falsity of Ideas," *The Philosophical Review*, 102:3 (July 1993), 309–34.
Fine, Gail. *On Ideas*. Oxford: Clarendon Press, 1993.
Friedman, Michael. "Descartes on the Real Existence of Matter," *Topoi*, 16:2 (1997), 153–62.
—. "Transcendental Philosophy and Mathematical Physics," *Studies in History and Philosophy of Science*, 34 (2003), 29–43.
Galileo. *Two New Sciences*, translated by Stillman Drake. Madison, WI: University of Wisconsin Press, 1974.
Garber, Daniel. *Descartes' Metaphysical Physics*. Chicago: Chicago University Press, 1992.
Gaukroger, Stephen. *Cartesian Logic*. Oxford: Clarendon Press, 1989.
—. *Descartes: An Intellectual Biography*. Oxford: Clarendon Press, 1995.
Gilbert, Neal. *Renaissance Concepts of Method*. New York: Columbia University Press, 1960.
Gorham, Geoffrey. "Descartes on Time and Duration," *Early Science and Medicine* 12 (2007), 28–54.
Grene, Margorie. *Descartes*. Minneapolis, MN: University of Minnesota Press, 1985.
Grosholtz, Emily. *Cartesian Method and the Problem of Reduction*. Oxford: Clarendon Press, 1991.
—. *Representation and Productive Ambiguity in Mathematics and the Sciences*. Oxford: Oxford University Press, 2007.
Grosseteste, Robert. *On Light*, translated by Clare Riedl. Milwaukee, WI: Marquette University Press, 1942.
Gueroult, Martial. *Descartes' Philosophy Interpreted According to the Order of Reasons*, translated by Roger Ariew, 2 vols. Minneapolis, MN: University of Minnesota Press, 1984.

Hatfield, Gary. "Descartes' Physiology and Its Relation to His Psychology," *The Cambridge Companion to Descartes*, edited by John Cottingham. Cambridge: Cambridge University Press, 1992.

Hillgarth, J. N. *Ramon Lull and Lullism in Fourteenth-Century France*. Oxford: The Clarendon Press, 1971.

Hintikka, Jaakko. "*Cogito, Ergo Sum*: Inference or Performance?" *The Philosophical Review*, 71:1 (January 1962), 3–32.

Hoffding, Harald. *A History of Modern Philosophy*, 2 vols, translated by B. E. Meyer. London: Macmillan & Co., 1924.

Hoffman, Paul. "The Unity of Descartes's Man," *The Philosophical Review*, 95:3 (July 1986), 339–70.

—. "Cartesian Passions and Cartesian Dualism," *Pacific Philosophical Quarterly*, 71 (1990), 310–33.

—. "Descartes on Misrepresentation," *Journal of the History of Philosophy*, XXXIV:3 (July 1996), 356–81.

—. "Direct Realism and the Objective Being of Ideas," *Pacific Philosophical Quarterly*, 83 (2002a), 163–79.

—. "Descartes's Theory of Distinction," *Philosophy and Phenomenological Research*, LXIV:1 (January 2002b), 57–78.

Hofmann, Joseph Ehrenfried. *Classical Mathematics*. New York: Barnes & Noble, 2003. Originally published by Philosophical Library, Inc., 1959.

Humber, James. "Clarity, Distinctness, the *Cogito*, and 'I,'" *Idealistic Studies*, XVII:1 (1987), 15–37.

Jardine, Lisa. "Humanism and the Teaching of Logic," *The Cambridge History of Later Medieval Philosophy*, edited by Norman Kretzmann, Anthony Kenny, and Jan Pinborg. Cambridge: Cambridge University Press, 1982.

Kant, Immanuel. *Critique of Pure Reason*, translated by Norman Kemp-Smith. New York: Bedford Books, 1969.

Kenny, Anthony. *Descartes: A Study of His Philosophy*. New York: Random House, 1968.

—. "Descartes on the Will," *Cartesian Studies*. Oxford: Basil Blackwell, 1972.

Knudsen, Christian. "Intentions and Impositions," *The Cambridge History of Later Medieval Philosophy*, edited by Norman Kretzmann, Anthony Kenny, and Jan Pinborg. Cambridge: Cambridge University Press, 1982.

Kremer, Elmar, "Antoine Arnauld," *The Stanford Encyclopedia of Philosophy* (Fall 2012 Edition), edited by Edward N. Zalta. URL = <http://plato.stanford.edu/archives/fall2012/entries/arnauld/>.

Lachterman, David R. "*Objectum Purae Matheseos*: Mathematical Construction and the Passage from Essence to Existence," *Essays on Descartes' Meditations*, edited by Amélie Oksenberg Rorty. Los Angeles, CA: University of California Press, 1986.

Lagerlund, Henrik and Yrjonsurri, Mikko (eds). *Emotions and Choice From Boethius to Descartes*. Dordrecht: Kluwer, 2002.

Lennon, Thomas M. "Representationalism, Judgment and Perception of Distance: Further to Yolton and McRae," *Dialogue*, 19:1 (1980) 151–62.

—. "Descartes' Idealism," *Philosophie et Culture*, vol. IV, Actes du XVIIe Congrès Mondial de Philosophie. Montreal: Editions de Beffroi, Editions Montmorency, 1986, pp. 53–6.

—. *The Battle of the Gods and Giants*. Princeton, NJ: Princeton University Press, 1993.

—. "The Eleatic Descartes," *Journal of the History of Philosophy*, 45:1 (2007), 29–45.

—. *The Plain Truth: Descartes, Huet, and Skepticism*. Leiden: Brill, 2008.

Locke, John. *An Essay Concerning Human Understanding*, edited by Peter H. Nidditch. Oxford: Clarendon Press, 1975.

MacKenzie, Ann. "The Reconfiguration of Sensory Experience," *Reason, Will, and Sensation*, edited by John Cottingham. Oxford: Clarendon Press, 1994.

—. "Descartes on Sensory Representation: A Study of the Dioptrics," *Canadian Journal of Philosophy*, Supplementary Volume 16 (1990), 109–47.

Malebranche, Nicolas. *Dialogues on Metaphysics*, translated by Willis Doney. New York: Abaris Books, 1980a.

—. *The Search After Truth*, translated by Thomas M. Lennon and Paul J. Olscamp. Columbus, OH: Ohio State University Press, 1980b.

Marion, Jean-Luc. "Cartesian Metaphysics and the Role of the Simple Natures," *The Cambridge Companion to Descartes*, edited by John Cottingham. Cambridge: Cambridge University Press, 1992.

McInerny, Ralph and O'Callaghan, John, "Saint Thomas Aquinas," *The Stanford Encyclopedia of Philosophy* (Winter 2013 Edition), edited by Edward N. Zalta. URL = <http://plato.stanford.edu/archives/win2013/entries/aquinas/>.

McMullin, Ernan (ed.). *The Concept of Matter in Modern Philosophy*. Notre Dame: University of Notre Dame Press, 1978.

McRae, Robert. Innate Ideas, *Cartesian Studies*, edited by R. J. Butler. Oxford: Basil Blackwell, 1972.

Mendelson, Michael. "Saint Augustine," *The Stanford Encyclopedia of Philosophy* (Winter 2012 Edition), edited by Edward N. Zalta. URL = <http://plato.stanford.edu/archives/win2012/entries/augustine/>.

Menn, Stephen. "The Greatest Stumbling Block: Descartes' Denial of Real Qualities," *Descartes and His Contemporaries*, edited by Roger Ariew and Marjorie Grene. Chicago: University of Chicago Press, 1995.

—. *Descartes and Augustine*. Cambridge: Cambridge University Press, 1998.

Moore, G. E. "Proof of an External World," *Philosophical Papers*, Chapter VII. London: George Allen & Unwin Ltd., 1959.

Nadler, Steven. *Arnauld and the Cartesian Philosophy of Ideas*. Manchester: Manchester University Press, 1989.
—. "Descartes and Occasional Causation," *British Journal of the History of Philosophy*, 2:1 (1994), 35–54.
Nelson, Alan. "Cartesian Actualism in the Leibniz–Arnauld Correspondence," *Canadian Journal of Philosophy*, 23:4 (December 1993), 675–94.
—. "The Falsity in Sensory Ideas: Descartes and Arnauld," *Interpreting Arnauld*, edited by Elmar Kremer. Toronto: University of Toronto Press, 1996.
—. "Descartes's Ontology of Thought," *Topoi*, 16 (1997), 163–78.
—. "Cartesian Innateness," *A Companion to Descartes*, edited by Janet Broughton and John Carriero. Malden, MA: Blackwell Publishers, 2008, pp. 319–33.
Newton, Isaac. *The Principia*, translated by Andrew Motte. Amherst, MA: Prometheus Books, 1995.
Nolan, Lawrence. "The Ontological Status of Cartesian Natures," *Pacific Philosophical Quarterly*, 78 (1997a), 169–94.
—. "Reductionism and Nominalism in Descartes's Theory of Attributes," *Topoi*, 10:2 (September 1997b), 129–40.
—. "The Role of the Imagination in Rationalist Philosophies of Mathematics," *A Companion to Rationalism*, edited by Alan Nelson. Oxford: Blackwell Publishing, 2005, pp. 224–49.
Normore, Calvin. "Meaning and Objective Being: Descartes and His Sources," *Essays on Descartes' Meditations*, edited by Amelie Oksenberg Rorty. Berkeley, CA: University of California Press, 1986.
Norton, David. *An Essential Contradiction in Descartes' Third Meditation*. MA Thesis, Claremont, CA: The Claremont Graduate School, 1964.
O'Neil, Brian. *Epistemological Direct Realism in Descartes' Philosophy*. Albuquerque, NM: University of New Mexico Press, 1974.
Ong, Walter. *Ramus: Method, and the Decay of Dialogue*. Cambridge, MA: Harvard University Press, 1958.
Osler, Margaret. "Divine Will and Mathematical Truth: Gassendi and Descartes on the Status of the Eternal Truths," *Descartes and His Contemporaries*, edited by Roger Ariew and Marjorie Grene. Chicago: University of Chicago Press, 1995.
O'Toole, Frederick. "Descartes' Problematic Causal Principle," *Descartes's Meditations*, edited by Vere Chappell. Lanham, MD: Rowman & Littlefield Publishers, 1997, pp. 103–28.
Popkin, Richard. *The History of Scepticism from Erasmus to Descartes*. Assen: Van Gorcum, 1960.
Randall, John. *The Career of Philosophy: From the Middle Ages to the Enlightenment*. New York: Columbia University Press, 1962.

Rorty, Amelie Oksenberg. "Descartes on Thinking with the Body," *The Cambridge Companion to Descartes*, edited by John Cottingham. Cambridge: Cambridge University Press, 1992.

Rozemond, Marleen. *Descartes's Dualism*. Cambridge, MA: Harvard University Press, 1998.

Rutherford, Donald. "Descartes' Ethics," *The Stanford Encyclopedia of Philosophy* (Spring 2013 Edition), edited by Edward N. Zalta. URL = <http://plato.stanford.edu/archives/spr2013/entries/descartes-ethics/>.

Ryle, Gilbert. *The Concept of Mind*. London: Hutchinson's University Library, 1949.

Schmaltz, Tad. "Spinoza on the Vacuum," *Archiv für Geschichte der Philosophie*, 81:2 (1999), 174–205.

—. *Descartes on Causation*. Oxford: Oxford University Press, 2007.

Sepper, Dennis. "Cartesian Imaginations: The Methods and Passions of Imagining," *A Companion to Rationalism*, edited by Alan Nelson. Oxford: Blackwell Publishers, 2005.

Slowik, Edward. "Descartes' Physics," *The Stanford Encyclopedia of Philosophy* (Fall 2013 Edition), edited by Edward N. Zalta. URL = <http://plato.stanford.edu/archives/fall2013/entries/descartes-physics/>.

Smith, Kurt. "A General Theory of Cartesian Clariy and Distinctness Based on the Theory of Enumeration in the *Rules*," *Dialogue*, XL:2 (Spring 2001), 279–310.

—. "Was Descartes's Physics Mathematical?" *History of Philosophy Quarterly*, 20:3 (July 2003), 245–56.

—. "Rationalism and Representation," *A Companion to Rationalism*, edited by Alan Nelson. Oxford: Blackwell Publishing, 2005a, pp. 206–23.

—. "Descartes's Ontology of Sensation," *Canadian Journal of Philosophy*, 35:4 (December 2005b), 563–84.

—. "Cartesian Substance and Divisibility," *Oxford Studies in Early Modern Philosophy*, vol. 5. Oxford: Clarendon Press, 2010a, pp. 1–24.

—. *Matter Matters: Metaphysics and Methodology in the Early Modern Period*. Oxford: Oxford University Press, 2010b.

—. "Descartes' Life and Works," *The Stanford Encyclopedia of Philosophy* (Fall 2012 Edition), edited by Edward N. Zalta. URL = <http://plato.stanford.edu/archives/fall2013/entries/descartes-works/>.

—. "Descartes' Theory of Ideas," *The Stanford Encyclopedia of Philosophy* (Spring 2013 Edition), edited by Edward N. Zalta. URL = <http://plato.stanford.edu/archives/spr2013/entries/descartes-ideas/>.

Smyth, Herbert. *Greek Grammar*, revised by Gordon Messing. Cambridge, MA: Harvard University Press, 1984.
Sorell, Tom. *Descartes*. Oxford: Oxford University Press, 1987.
Sowaal, Alice. "Cartesian Bodies," *Canadian Journal of Philosophy*, 34:2 (2004), 217–40.
—. "Idealism and Cartesian Motion," *A Companion to Rationalism*,' edited by Alan Nelson (Oxford: Blackwell Publishers, 2005), pp. 250–61.
Spinoza, Benedict. *Ethics*, translated by A. H. Stirling. Hertfordshire: Wordsworth Editions, 2001.
Suarez, Francisco. "On Efficient Causality," *Metaphysical Disputations: 17, 18, and 19*, translated by Alfred Freddoso. New Haven, CT: Yale University Press, 1994.
Weinberg, Julius. "Ideas and Concepts," *The Aquinas Lecture*. Milwaukee, WI: Marquette University Press, 1970.
Wells, Norman. "Material Falsity in Descartes, Arnauld, and Suarez," *Journal of the History of Philosophy*, XXII:1 (January 1984), 25–50.
—. "Objective Reality of Ideas in Descartes, Caterus, and Suarez," *The Journal of the History of Philosophy*, XXVIII:1 (January 1990), 33–61.
Williams, Bernard. *Descartes: The Project of Pure Enquiry*. New York: Penguin, 1990. Published earlier by Pelican Books, 1978.
Wilson, Catherine. "Leibniz and the Animalcula," *Oxford Studies in the History of Philosophy*, edited by M. A. Stewart. Oxford: Clarendon Press, 1997, pp. 153–75.
Wilson, Margaret. *Descartes*. London: Routledge & Kegan Paul, 1978.
—. "Descartes on Sense and 'Resemblance,'" *Reason, Will, and Sensation*, edited by John Cottingham. Oxford: Clarendon Press, 1994.
Yates, Frances. *Lull & Bruno*, vol. 1. London: Routledge & Kegan Paul, 1982.
Yolton, John. *Perceptual Acquaintance from Descartes to Reid*. Minneapolis, MN: University of Minnesota Press, 1984.
—. "Representation and Realism: Some Reflections on the Way of Ideas," *Mind* XCVI:383 (1987), 318–30.

www.ingramcontent.com/pod-product-compliance
Ingram Content Group UK Ltd.
Pitfield, Milton Keynes, MK11 3LW, UK
UKHW021834220426
470268UK00007B/152